ECONOMIZATION OF EDUCATION

D0206826

In this timely, cogent analysis of trends and powerful forces shaping global educational policy today, Joel Spring focuses on how economization is making economic growth and increased productivity the main goals of schools, and the ways these goals are achieved—including measuring educational policies by their costs and economic benefits, shaping family life to ensure productive workers and high-achieving students, introducing entrepreneurship education into curricula from preschool through higher education, and increasing the involvement of economists in educational policy analysis. Close attention is given to the Organization for Economic Cooperation and Development (OECD), the World Bank, the World Economic Forum, and multinational corporations, which, as advocates of economization, want schools to focus on teaching hard and soft skills needed by the global labor market.

Economization raises questions about the effects of economically driven agendas for schools: Will education policies advocated by global organizations and multinational businesses corporatize and standardize human personalities and families? What type of global worker is being sought by global organizations and multinational corporations? What education programs are supported to educate the ideal global worker? What is the ideal family life for economic growth and development? Detailing and analyzing the politics and motivations driving economization, the book concludes with an assessment of the impacts of the confluence of business interests, economic theories, governments, and educators.

Joel Spring is Professor at Queens College/City University of New York and the Graduate Center of the City University of New York, USA.

Sociocultural, Political, and Historical Studies in Education
Joel Spring, Editor

Spring • *Wheels in the Head: Educational Philosophies of Authority, Freedom, and Culture from Confucianism to Human Rights, Third Edition*

Spring • *The Intersection of Cultures: Global Multicultural Education, Fourth Edition*

Gabbard, Ed. • *Knowledge and Power in the Global Economy: The Effects of School Reform in a Neoliberal/Neoconservative Age, Second Edition*

Spring • *A New Paradigm for Global School Systems: Education for a Long and Happy Life*

Books, Ed. • *Invisible Children in the Society and Its Schools, Third Edition*

Spring • *Pedagogies of Globalization: The Rise of the Educational Security State*

Sidhu • *Universities and Globalization: To Market, To Market*

Bowers/Apffel-Marglin, Eds. • *Rethinking Freire: Globalization and the Environmental Crisis*

Reagan • *Non-Western Educational Traditions: Indigenous Approaches to Educational Thought and Practice, Third Edition*

Books • *Poverty and Schooling in the U.S.: Contexts and Consequences*

Shapiro/Purpel, Eds. • *Critical Social Issues in American Education: Democracy and Meaning in a Globalizing World, Third Edition*

Spring • *How Educational Ideologies are Shaping Global Society: Intergovernmental Organizations, NGOs, and the Decline of the Nation-State*

Lakes/Carter, Eds. • *Global Education for Work: Comparative Perspectives on Gender and the New Economy*

Heck • *Studying Educational and Social Policy: Theoretical Concepts and Research Methods*

Peshkin • *Places of Memory: Whiteman's Schools and Native American Communities*

Hemmings • *Coming of Age in U.S. High Schools: Economic, Kinship, Religious, and Political Crosscurrents*

Spring • *Educating the Consumer-Citizen: A History of the Marriage of Schools, Advertising, and Media*

Ogbu • *Black American Students in an Affluent Suburb: A Study of Academic Disengagement*

Benham/Stein, Eds. • *The Renaissance of American Indian Higher Education: Capturing the Dream*

Hones, Ed. • *American Dreams, Global Visions: Dialogic Teacher Research with Refugee and Immigrant Families*

McCarty • *A Place to Be Navajo: Rough Rock and The Struggle for Self-Determination in Indigenous Schooling*

Spring • *Globalization and Educational Rights: An Intercivilizational Analysis*

Grant/Lei, Eds. • *Global Constructions of Multicultural Education: Theories and Realities*

Luke • *Globalization and Women in Academics: North/West–South/East*

Meyer/Boyd, Eds. • *Education Between State, Markets, and Civil Society: Comparative Perspectives*

Roberts • *Remaining and Becoming: Cultural Crosscurrents in an Hispano School*

For additional information on titles in the Sociocultural, Political, and Historical Studies in Education series visit **www.routledge.com/education**.

ECONOMIZATION OF EDUCATION

Human Capital, Global Corporations, Skills-Based Schooling

Joel Spring

 Routledge
Taylor & Francis Group

NEW YORK AND LONDON

First published 2015
by Routledge
711 Third Avenue, New York, NY 10017

and by Routledge
2 Park Square, Milton Park, Abingdon, Oxon, OX14 4RN

Routledge is an imprint of the Taylor & Francis Group, an informa business

Library of Congress Cataloging in Publication Data
Spring, Joel H.
Economization of education : human capital, global corporations,
skills-based schooling/by Joel Spring.
pages cm
Includes bibliographical references and index.
1. Education—Economic aspects. 2. Corporatization—United States.
3. Human capital. 4. Educational sociology. 5. Education and globalization.
I. Title.
LC65.S66 2015
338.4′7374013—dc23
2014041455

ISBN: 978-1-138-84460-5 (hbk)
ISBN: 978-1-138-84461-2 (pbk)
ISBN: 978-1-315-73023-3 (ebk)

Typeset in Bembo
by Swales & Willis Ltd, Exeter, Devon, UK

Printed and bound in the United States of America by Publishers Graphics,
LLC on sustainably sourced paper.

CONTENTS

PREFACE

I began this book wondering why there are so many economists involved in educational research and policy. I was startled by claims that test scores could predict a country's future economic growth and that skills were the new currency of the global economy. In the US many schools had already adopted a skills-based curriculum called the Common Core State Standards and globally schools were being ranked by student performance on the Organization for Economic Cooperation's international test PISA. It didn't make sense to me that policy-makers would declare that investment in education would grow and improve an economy when the up-and-down swings in the global economy are caused by events other than the quality of schools.

I trace the influence of economic theories on education back to the 1940s and 1950s and the Chicago School of Economics. As I explain in Chapter 1, it was this school of economic thought that promulgated theories about the economic importance of human capital and the idea that education could grow the economy. Using rational choice theory, some of these Chicago economists applied economic theories to every aspect of human life. The ideas of the Chicago School of Economics appeared in the early work of the Organization for Economic Cooperation and Development (OECD), the World Bank and the World Economic Forum.

As explained in Chapter 2, the OECD was the first global organization to use human capital economics to develop education policies and to call on nations to invest in skills-based curricula. Their policy statements claim that investing in education causes economic growth and reduces inequalities in income. However, human capital economists don't think school credentials and years-of-schooling are accurate measurements of education's economic impact. Consequently, economists wanted to identify the skills learned in schools that contribute to worker performance and economic growth. By the 1990s, OECD developed

PISA to measure skills related to employment and the world began to jump on the skills-based education bandwagon.

As detailed in Chapter 3, surveys of global businesses indicated the hard and soft skills wanted by employers. Hard skills refer primarily to literacy and mathematics along with specific skills for a particular occupation. Soft skills refer to workers' behaviors, such as conscientiousness, team work, and a work ethic. Consequently, OECD initiated a survey of adult skills (PIAAC) and the World Bank developed the Step Skills Measurement Program. These tests, combined with PISA and the math and science test TIMSS, were to measure the quality of a country's human capital. This initiated a world Olympiad of test scores with national schools ranked on a comparative scale.

As explained in Chapter 4, the World Bank adopted the human capital ideas of the Chicago School of Economics and lent money to developing nations to improve their schools as a means of stimulating the economy. The World Bank's policies also pressed for improved education to eliminate world poverty.

The World Economic Forum, discussed in Chapter 5, representing the world's richest corporations, readily pushed for a skills-based education. The previously discussed tests were used in determining its Human Capital Report and Human Capital Index as measures of the quality of a nation's workforce. The World Economic Forum advocated closer ties between businesses in formulating education policies and introduced entrepreneurship education as another economic solution for poverty and income inequality while repeating the mantra that education could grow the economy, end poverty, and reduce income inequalities.

Worried about families teaching the "right" soft skills for school success and employment, some economists and sociologists turned their attention to family interactions. Consequently, as described in Chapter 6, these economists and sociologists advocated particular family structures to ensure the passing on of the "right" soft skills. Their position is that if the family fails in this endeavor, then preschool is to compensate. James Heckman, a Chicago School of Economics member, argued that preschools should be organized to teach the soft skills needed for success in further schooling and employment.

Missing from work-oriented soft skills are those that might lead to struggles for social justice and a pushing back against corporate control; soft skills such as compassion, altruism, and empathy. Reflecting the corporate-serving nature of their arguments, Chicago economist Gary Becker argued that altruism makes families efficient while selfishness makes markets efficient. The result is corporatized schools and the economization of the behavior and attitudes of corporate workers.

Finally, in Chapter 7 I argue that these trends have resulted in an economization of schools, families, and character development in which the ideal social interactions within the family are to support the work of the breadwinners and prepare children for success in school and later employment. This economization and corporatization of families and schools is not a conspiracy but a confluence of interests between global businesses, politicians, governments, and education policymakers.

1

ECONOMIZATION AND CORPORATIZATION OF EDUCATION

In his 1992 Nobel Prize acceptance lecture, economist Gary Becker said, "My research uses the economic approach to analyze social issues that range beyond those usually considered by economists."[1] The title of the lecture, "The Economic Way of Looking at Life," captured Becker's pioneering work in applying economic models to a host of social issues, including the family, crime, discrimination, and, most importantly for this book, education. Becker's 1964 book *Human Capital* continues to influence governments and global policymaking organizations with its message to invest in education to grow the economy.[2]

Becker was a member of what became known as the Chicago School of Economics,[i] which included other Nobel Prize winners who applied economics to education, such as Milton Friedman, Theodore Schultz, and James Heckman. Associated with this group at the University of Chicago was sociologist James Coleman who contributed theoretical frameworks on social capital and rational choice to the economization of education.

Historically, human capital and the application of free market economics to public education received their greatest support from the Chicago School. In fact, ideas emanating from the Chicago School still infuse global education policies. The global importance of the Chicago School is captured in the title of Johan Van Overtveldt's *The Chicago School: How the University of Chicago Assembled the Thinkers who Revolutionized Economics and Business.*[3] The Chicago School and its followers not only revolutionized thinking about economics, but also global education policies.

Economization refers to the increasing involvement of economists in education research, the evaluation of the effectiveness of schools and family life

i. To be referred to in this chapter as the "Chicago School."

according to cost/benefit analyses, and the promotion of school choice in a competitive marketplace. The Chicago School's application of economic reasoning to everyday life results in measuring the contribution of family life and schools to economic growth and productivity. This general attempt to apply economic reasoning to all aspects of life is captured in the title of the 1997 publication of Gary Becker's popular *Business Week* columns, *The Economics of Life: From Baseball to Affirmative Action to Immigration, How Real-World Issues Affect Our Everyday Life.*[4]

The application of choice or free market thinking to education can be attributed to the work of Becker's mentor Milton Friedman. Friedman introduced the ideas of school choice in a paper published in 1955 and then used the term "vouchers" for funding school choice in his now famous 1962 book, *Capitalism and Freedom.*[5] Friedman contributed to Becker's efforts, and that of other economists, to apply economic reasoning to everyday life. In a volume dedicated to remembering the University of Chicago faculty, Becker described the influence of Friedman's teaching: "The emphasis in his course on applications of theory to the real world set the tone of the department."[6]

Becker and Friedman's application of market principles to education had a lasting impact on the language of education, introducing terms such as competition, investment, consumer choice, for-profit schools, vouchers, economic progress, and global free trade in educational services. Friedman advocated school choice, vouchers, and for-profit education using economic phrases such as "vocational training . . . increases economic productivity";[7] "schooling adds to the economic value of the student";[8] "the 'education industry'";[9] and "vocational and professional schooling . . . is a form of investment in human capital precisely analogous to investment in machinery, buildings."[10] Written for the general public, *Free to Choose: A Personal Statement,* coauthored with his wife Rose Friedman, refers to students as "consumers";[11] teachers as "producers";[12] colleges as "selling schooling";[13] colleges as producing and selling "monuments and research";[14] higher education as improving "economic productivity of individuals";[15] and colleges providing an "incentive" to attend by offering an opportunity for "higher earnings."[16]

Similar economic language applied to education can be found in the work of the pioneer in human capital, economist Theodore Schultz. In his 1963 classic work, *The Economic Value of Education,* he referred to schools as "firms" that "specialize in producing schooling."[17] He also called the educational establishment "an industry" that makes "production" decisions.[18] Schultz portrayed student actions in economic terms: "Suppose, then, that all of the costs of schooling are charged to the investment in the production capabilities of students."[19]

Gary Becker would influence public views of education as an economic enterprise by referring in his 1964 book *Human Capital* to schooling as "Investment in Human Capital" with estimates on "the money rate of return to college and high-school education in the United States."[20] In Becker's writings, as I describe later, education becomes an investment that results in economic growth, increased productivity, higher incomes, decreased economic inequalities, and the ending of poverty.

Human Capital, Free Markets, and Economization

An important part of the Chicago School's tradition, as reflected in the work of Friedman, Schultz, Becker, and Heckman, is the consideration of schooling as an investment in human capital. For my purposes, I am using the definition of human capital given in *The Oxford Handbook of Human Capital*: "The stock of knowledge and skills that enables people to perform work that creates economic value."[21]

The concept of human capital can be traced back to Adam Smith's *The Wealth of Nations* (1776) when Smith wrote about a person's talents as "a capital fixed and realized, as it were, in his person."[22] After World War II, the Cold War between the Soviet Union and the US pushed the concept of human capital to the forefront. Almost immediately following WWII, US policymakers began to worry about having the knowledge resources to win the military-technology race with the Soviet Union. As a result, the National Science Foundation was created in 1950 to ensure a supply of scientists, engineers, and mathematicians and to sponsor research. In addition, national manpower planning was formally instituted with the passage of the 1951 Universal Military and Training Act requiring military service for all men with deferments from military service for those attending college and for those holding jobs considered important for national defense. The purpose of college and occupational deferments from military service was explained by Anna Rosenberg, the assistant secretary of the Department of Defense, to the Senate Committee considering the legislation: "We feel . . . that with our shortage of manpower it is essential that we make it up in skills; that the skilled manpower, the scientific manpower, the highly trained manpower is essential for the national interest."[23]

As members of the Chicago School researched the effect of human capital on the economy, the 1957 launching of Soviet Sputnik I created a demand by many politicians for more scientists and engineers to keep pace with Soviet technological advances. Reacting to the Soviet accomplishments in space, President Dwight Eisenhower said in 1957 that the problem facing the US was graduating more scientists and engineers to match the numbers that were graduating from Soviet schools. Eisenhower asserted that "My scientific advisers place this problem above all other immediate tasks of producing missiles . . . [we need] to stimulate good-quality teaching of mathematics and science."[24] The result was Congressional passage of the 1958 National Defense Education Act which provided funds to attract students into the fields of science, engineering, and math.[25]

The Cold War also sent a wave of anti-communism through public schools and universities. The anti-Communist movement in universities favored economists advocating free markets and who relied on mathematical methods. Prior to

WWII, US economists tended to work from a variety of ideological positions. Economic historian Craufurd Goodwin wrote about this transition: "It is difficult for the present-day academic economist, accustomed to teaching mainly the . . . wonders of the free market system, to appreciate that not long ago this discipline was widely feared as the seat of radicalism."[26]

After WWII, university leaders were afraid to hire professors identified with the political left, or even liberal intellectuals, who might be accused of being Communist or Communist sympathizers. Consequently, universities favored economists who espoused free market principles like those advocated by the Chicago School. In addition, economists strove to be "scientific" so that they could not be accused of ideological interpretations of the functioning of the economy. The use of mathematics became central to economic research after WWII because it appeared ideologically neutral. For instance, Gary Becker's research on human capital is punctuated with elaborate mathematical formulas. However, as I will discuss, this did not result in completely objective conclusions by Milton Friedman or Gary Becker or other economists of the period. As two economic historians assert, "the tool-kit style of postwar economics . . . could be used to disguise theoretical content and ideology to the outside world."[27]

In public schools progressive education was labeled "Communist" and there were calls for a return to the "basics."[28] Along with anti-Communism and a desire to graduate more scientists and engineers, the post-WWII civil rights movement struggled against school segregation laws. By the 1960s, the civil rights movement focused increasingly on the issue of poverty along with racial equality. A result was the War on Poverty program of President Lyndon B. Johnson's administration which stressed increased educational opportunities as a solution to poverty. The War on Poverty contained human capital arguments that investment in education would grow the economy, eliminate poverty, and reduce income inequalities. The 1964 Annual Report of the Council of Economic Advisers, "The Problem of Poverty in America," claimed, "Equality of Opportunity is the American dream, and universal education our noblest pledge to realize it. But, for the children of the poor, education is a handicap race; many are too *ill motivated at home to learn in school* [author's emphasis]."[29] This statement foreshadowed the increasing concerns by economists with changing family life to prepare children for school so that the economy would grow and poverty would disappear.

Anti-Communism, fears generated by the military-technological race with the Soviet Union, and concerns about poverty contributed to the dominant role in education of the Chicago School's ideas about free markets and human capital. In 1961, Theodore Schultz noted the importance of human capital: "economists have long known that people are an important part of the wealth of nations."[30] Schultz argued that people invested in themselves through education to improve their job opportunities. In his 1964 book on human capital, Gary Becker asserted that economic growth now depended on the knowledge, information, ideas, skills, and health of the workforce. Investments in education, he argued, could improve human capital which would contribute to economic growth.[31]

Human capital arguments contributed to thinking about education as primarily an economic activity. Knowledge and skills learned in school were capital to be utilized in economic activity. Workers with high levels of skills and knowledge acquired through education and experience are enabled "to produce more with the same inputs of land, machines, materials, and time than other workers without those traits."[32] This line of reasoning resulted in calls for schools to teach the knowledge and skills that increase economic growth and productivity. From a cost/benefit perspective, the benefits from educational investments outweigh the costs by increasing personal income and economic productivity and growth.

Global businesses and organizations representing their interests support the idea of the human capital approach to education because, as I explain in more detail throughout this volume, it emphasizes teaching skills needed in the workplace. In this context, human capital goals for education trump other educational goals, such as education for social justice, environmental improvement, political participation, and citizenship training.

Corporatization of Education and Families

Economic education goals result in corporatization of future workers by attempting to shape their character traits, knowledge, and skills to meet the needs of the global labor market and the desires of multinational corporations. In the context of human capital, skills are divided into hard and soft with hard skills usually referring to such things as literacy instruction and numeracy and soft skills to character traits that will help the worker succeed in the workplace.

The corporatization of the global worker is accompanied by attempts to corporatize the family so that family life ensures that workers in the family remain productive and that their children are prepared to learn the hard and soft skills needed to enhance their human capital and fit the employment needs of corporations. As I explain later in the book, the corporatization of the worker and the family introduces another form of capital, namely social capital. Social capital, in this context, refers to the contribution of social interactions to economic growth and productivity. Applied to education, social capital refers to the teaching of soft skills that will prepare the student for productive social interactions within corporations. Applied to the family, social capital refers to the relationships that affect the human capital of household members, particularly workers and children. For those arguing education is important for economic growth and employment, a dysfunctional family has a negative impact on a child's success in school and later employment, and reduces a child's human capital. The same argument can be extended to a child's peer group. Will a child's social relations contribute to school success and consequently increase economic growth and productivity?

In the following section I will highlight the concept of the economization and corporatization of education and the family by discussing a dystopian view of the future. Then I will discuss the origins of the economization of education by members of the Chicago School. The origin of the current global emphasis on education for growing the economy and teaching skills needed by multinational corporations can be found in the free market ideas and application of economics to education and people's behavior by the members of the Chicago School.

A Dystopian Vision of Corporate Control of Schools and Family Life

Let us consider the most extreme example of corporatization of education and family life before explicating the ideas underpinning economization, human capital, free markets, and for-profit schooling. This example will serve to highlight the present direction of global education and will illustrate the potential outcomes of educational economization. Patrick Flanery's novel *Fallen Land* depicts an imaginary global corporation called EKK that offers for-profit services covering all aspects of life including for-profit charter schools. The corporate offering of for-profit charter schools illustrates free market ideas applied to education. Also, EKK shows the potential of the free market to profit from every aspect of human life. EKK sells services from conception "to death and disposal (cremation, organ and tissue recycling, human remains management)."[33] EKK's corporate divisions, besides their charter school division, offer for-profit services including fertility and biotech, health care and medical subcontracting, charter school administration, curriculum development, universities, employment and employee relations, financial and assets management, security and incarceration, immigration and detention centers, entertainment, travel, hotel and resort management, and old age care. In other words, all parts of a citizen's life are objects of profit.

Illustrating the attempt to align family actions with corporate productivity, EKK provides its employees with a home protection system which monitors not only for fire and burglary, but also uses surveillance cameras to ensure that family life supports the productivity of adult workers and that their children are prepared to learn the hard and soft skills needed to succeed in school and the corporate workplace. In other words, family members are protected against family interactions or behavior traits that might harm their ability to be efficient corporate workers and students. The home protection system reports back to EKK any household or individual behaviors detrimental to the good of corporate life.

Flanery describes this corporate control of family life:

> Imagine wedding motion sensors to surveillance optics, so that technics of a given security system work not just to identify intruders, but also and not exclusively to monitor the health and wellbeing of the citizens it is

employed to protect. So . . . what then becomes possible is a holistic analysis of domestic health, climate, spending, energy and food consumption, sleep patterns, work patterns, brand preference, time allocation, interpersonal activity, hygiene, nutrition . . . [so] that people will . . . live better, healthier, safer, more *productive lives* [author's emphasis].[34]

Charter schools operated by EKK use monetary methods to instill corporate discipline. A newly hired employee is informed that he is expected to enroll his child in the corporation's for-profit charter school called the Pinwheel Academy. The school's guidance counselor explains to new students that it operates on a system of disciplinary fines. Each student has an individualized account linked to their fingerprints. Money deposited in the account by parents is used for lunch and field trips, and for paying fines, such as $5 for being tardy to school, $25 for every detention, and $40 a day for unexcused absences.[35] Classrooms are tightly controlled with surveillance cameras whirling overhead, students and teachers wear uniforms, and students are not allowed to talk to each other during class and bathroom breaks. For bathroom breaks, students stand next to their desks and then leave the classroom in orderly lines. Row monitors observe students as they return and enter the classroom in groups of five. Any talking on reentering the classroom is, of course, fined. At lunch time, student fingerprints are scanned and lunch costs are debited to their individual accounts. The lunchroom and play areas are tightly controlled by security guards wearing hats with EKK's corporate logo. When a fight breaks out on the playground, security guards use tasers to separate students. Classroom lessons are conducted in the same authoritarian manner.[36]

The Pinwheel Academy is Patrick Flanery's vision of a charter school preparing corporate workers through stringent methods of behavioral control. In contrast, as I will explain later, surveys have found that global corporations want workers to have soft skills related to teamwork. Teamwork is clearly absent from Flanery's dystopian charter school. Of course, the Pinwheel Academy only represents one novelist's vision of the future.

The Rational Choice Paradigm and Economization

The rational choice paradigm is central to arguments by Milton Friedman for freedom in the marketplace and education vouchers, and for Theodore Shultz and Gary Becker's theory of human capital. The assumption of the rational choice paradigm is that humans act according to their calculation of costs and benefits. This is a highly individualistic concept of humans. Group activity is considered a result of people deciding that working with others is in their own self-interest. As part of the economization of education, it is assumed that parents weigh cost and benefits of spending money on their children's education and that college age students weigh the cost and benefits before investing in higher education.

Shultz called calculation of education investments, the "Arithmetic of Schooling and Growth."[37]

Prior to WWI and the influence of the Chicago School, two strands of thought reflected the pluralism of ideas among economists. Some economists focused on the public good with their work reflecting the social gospel movement and socialist movements. Some economists wrote about social reform issues and how government could act to improve the lives of all. There was also an efficiency movement related to scientific management, in which some economists examined how businesses could become more productive.[38]

After WWII, economists concerned with promoting the public good, in contrast to the individualism of the marketplace, were often accused of being Communists. This was exemplified by William F. Buckley Jr.'s 1951 book *God and Man at Yale: The Superstitions of "Academic Freedom"*, which criticized Yale's economics department for not stressing the importance of the individual over the collective good:

> If the recent Yale graduate, who exposed himself to Yale economics during his undergraduate years, exhibits enterprise, self-reliance, and independence, it is only because he has turned his back upon his teachers and texts. It is because he has not hearkened to those who assiduously disparage the individual, glorify the government, enshrine security, and discourage self-reliance.[39]

Buckley argued that the traditions of the Yale economics department were leading to a decline of individual power and an increase of government power "through extended social services, taxation, and regulation.[40] The Chicago School advocated the reduction of government's role in all three of these government functions as it took its stand against collectivism and Communism.

The rational choice paradigm appeared ideologically neutral and emphasized individualism, consequently it escaped accusations of being Communist. Gary Becker's *A Treatise on the Family* provides an example of how economists used the rational choice paradigm to evaluate education programs.[41] Published in 1981, Becker chided University of California psychologist Arthur Jensen for claiming that compensatory education programs for so-called disadvantaged children fail because of the low intelligence scores of African Americans. Becker didn't disagree with Jensen that compensatory education fails to achieve its objective but he offered an alternative interpretation using rational choice paradigm with families treated as individuals who weigh costs and benefits. Public expenditures on compensatory education redistribute resources to some low-income children which, Becker reasoned, "induces parents concerned with equity to redistribute time and other expenditures away from these children toward other children or themselves."[42] In other words, families supposedly make a rational choice to decrease money and attention spent on their children who are participating in compensatory education because these children are having extra resources spent on them by the government. In Becker's words, "the main effect of the programs [compensatory education] is probably a redistribution of family expenditures away from their children [that are] participating . . . . What Jensen and others failed to realize is that family time and other resources would be allocated away from participating children to siblings and parents."[43]

A reliance on the rational choice paradigm can obscure other factors that might affect outcomes and create a myopic view of social phenomena. In the case of the failure of compensatory education, Becker does qualify his conclusion with the words "is probably." However, Becker offers no data to show that, in fact, families shift their resources to children not participating in compensatory education programs. It often happens, as I will explain in later examples, that those arguing from the rational choice paradigm interpret data without providing any evidence that their conclusions are true. A good example is my later discussion of the use of income data to conclude that education and economic growth will reduce inequalities in income. In the case of Becker's interpretation of the supposed failure of compensatory education, the focus is on family choices without consideration of other possible issues, such as the government administration of compensatory education programs, the social and economic conditions of families being served, the quality of teachers and administrators, the condition of schools offering the programs, etc.

The rational choice paradigm was criticized at a 1985 University of Chicago conference bringing together economists and psychologists, with papers being published in *Rational Choice: The Contrast between Economics and Psychology*.[44] As the reader can imagine, defining "rational" and "rationality" was an area of contention with multiple interpretations being given. The editors of the volume claim that the rational choice paradigm provides economics with a unified theory lacking in psychology and that economists think about market level behavior while psychologists are concerned with mental processes. Also, the editors argued, economists focus on data and price-benefit relations, while psychologists focus on the mental processing of data.[45]

To exemplify the differences between an economist using the rational choice paradigm and psychologists, the editors of the 1985 Chicago conference papers examined the statement, "There cannot be any money lying in the street, because someone else would have picked it up already." The editors write about this statement,

> For the economist operating within the rational choice paradigm this statement can be taken to mean that, for all practical purposes, the world behaves as if there were no money lying in the street. The psychologist, however, has no reasons to accept this statement as a working hypothesis. Instead, he or she would accept the possibility that some money may be lying in the street and would consider it worth learning who finds it and how.[46]

At the Chicago conference the most vocal critic of Gary Becker's use of the rational choice paradigm to evaluate the supposed failure of compensatory education was fellow economist Herbert Simon. In his original analysis, Becker had compared family reaction to compensatory education to public health programs. When public health programs are made available to families, families spend less of their money on health matters. Becker used the findings on public health programs to assert that families would do the same thing if public funds were used for compensatory education. Herbert Simon criticized Becker's lack of evidence that families actually acted in this manner regarding compensatory education programs. One should not apply the rational choice paradigm to predict outcomes, Simon asserted, without having any actual proof that the prediction is true.[47]

In another example, Simon criticized Becker for stating that "the major cause of these changes [in family organization between the 1940s and 1980s] is the growth in the earning power of women as the American economy developed."[48] Applying the rational choice paradigm, Becker argued that women made a rational economic choice to enter the workforce because of rising wages after WWII. As a result, women had fewer children (staying at home and not earning money increases the cost of children) and divorce rates increased as women became more economically independent. Becker concluded, "Greater labor force participation of women would itself raise the earning power of women and thereby reinforce the effects of economic development. Women invest more in market skills [for instance improving their human capital through education] and experiences when they spend a larger fraction of their time in market activities."[49]

Simon criticized Becker for relying only on income data to explain the increased participation of women in the labor force. Simon contended that the reductionist quality and narrowness of the rational choice paradigm results in not exploring other possible causes rooted in changes in American history, culture, and industrial organization. He argues that the true explanation for increased participation of women in the labor force "will be obtained not by raising the sophistication of the economic reasoning but only by painstaking examination of occupations in manufacturing and service industries and an even more difficult empirical examination of changes in women's attitudes about where they prefer to work."[50]

Simon's criticisms go to the heart of problems with the rational choice paradigm, namely neglecting social, political, and historical contexts. As I explain later, human capital studies of changes in income and education are interpreted as resulting from individual calculations made over time. The lack of concern about context in the rational choice paradigm is extremely important since early human capital arguments relied on income data from the early twentieth century to after WWII, which encompasses a period of two world wars and a major world depression. Surely these events affected changes in income and education. As I explain later, neglecting these historical changes human capital economists distorted their conclusions, resulting in convincing others that investing in education will create economic growth and reduce income inequalities.

Rational Choice, Milton Friedman, and Education Vouchers

After completing his Ph.D. at Columbia University in 1946, Milton Friedman joined the economics department at the University of Chicago where Frank Knight had already opened the modern discussion of price theory in a 1933 book on economic organization. Knight identified that a central problem of economic systems was how decisions were made about what goods and services should be produced and in what proportions. Knight identified two extremes in determining what goods and services to produce. On the one hand, decisions about production could be centrally planned and, on the other hand, they could be made by individual choice in a free market.[51] In the context of a government-operated school system, Friedman would contend that decisions about what knowledge should be taught to students is determined by public officials, while in a competitive education marketplace decisions would be made by consumers through the exercise of individual choice.

Besides advocating for individual choice in a free market, Friedman used the rational choice paradigm to predict that individuals will invest in their education by taking out loans to attend college because they calculate that a college education will increase their future incomes. Milton Friedman describes as a rational decision for individuals to invest in their own human capital, including schooling and job training, when it raises their productivity and they are then "rewarded in a free enterprise society by receiving a higher return for . . . services than . . . would otherwise be able to command."[52] Foreshadowing the future reliance on student loans in contrast to government providing free higher education, Friedman proposed in a 1962 publication that a lender advance a student funds "needed to finance his training on condition that he agree to pay the lender a specified fraction of his future earnings."[53]

During the time Friedman made his proposal to turn public education over to the forces of the marketplace, public education was in turmoil as the civil rights movement struggled to end racial segregation. The 1954 US Supreme Court decision *Brown vs. the Board of Education* ended legal segregation in Southern schools. The civil rights movement reflected a belief that government should act to protect the public good in contrast to individual choice in the marketplace.[54] As I will explain, the 1954 school desegregation decision posed a problem for Friedman because it highlighted how vouchers might lead to a continuation of racial segregation through parental choice plans.

The reliance on government to protect the common good would become part of the educational programs of the War on Poverty in the 1960s. By the twenty-first century concern with the public good would mostly disappear in a flood of educational legislation favoring charter schools, for-profit school management companies, and investing in education to increase individual incomes, spur economic growth, and reduce income inequalities. Discussions of education for social justice, citizenship and environmental education, and improving social conditions would be overwhelmed by demands that education focus on economic growth and increasing incomes. Concerns about the social good would almost disappear from the educational rhetoric of politicians.

Friedman's commitment to letting market forces determine the production of goods and services, such as education, was strengthened a year after joining the Chicago faculty when he participated with Friedrich von Hayek in the first meeting of the Mont Pelerin Society near Montreux, Switzerland in 1947 along with 36 other scholars. The Mont Pelerin Society still promotes free market economics and on its current website it shows a photo with the caption: "Milton Friedman (in light coat and with hat, in the center) with friends in an excursion at the first meeting of the Mont Pelerin Society in 1947."[55] The stated historical purpose of the Mont Pelerin Society as given on its website is: "Its sole objective was to facilitate an exchange of ideas between like-minded scholars in the hope of strengthening the principles and *practice of a free society and to study the workings, virtues, and defects of market-oriented economic systems* [author's emphasis]."[56]

One of the founders of the Pelerin Society, Friedrich von Hayek, joined Milton Friedman on the University of Chicago faculty in 1950 as Professor of Social and Moral Science on the Committee on Social Thought. According to the historian of the Chicago School, Hayek was not hired by the economics department because the members thought Hayek's book *The Road to Serfdom* was "too popular a work for a respectable scholar to perpetrate."[57] Originally published in 1944, *The Road to Serfdom* became a best seller and appeared in *Reader's Digest* as a condensed book. In 1945, Hayek did a lecture tour promoting the free market ideas and anti-totalitarian message of the book. While Hayek and Friedman disagreed on the extent of the application of scientific methods to economics, they shared a commitment to the free market.[58]

Reflecting his dislike for the totalitarianism of the Soviet Union and Nazi Germany, Hayek engaged in a discussion of price theory by arguing that centrally planned economies would eventually fail because of the difficulty of determining prices or the value of goods. According to Hayek, the value of goods in a free market is determined by individual choices while in a centrally planned economy it is determined by the interests of bureaucrats. What criterion is used by a government bureaucracy? Hayek's answer was that the inevitable criterion is one that promotes the personal interests and advantages of bureaucracy members. Bureaucrats and intellectuals supported by a bureaucracy, he argued, will advance social theories that vindicate the continued existence and expansion of the bureaucracy.[59]

Friedman also worried about government bureaucracies determining what should be produced at what price. In Friedman's proposed voucher system, what is valued is determined by parental choice in a competitive marketplace. For instance, how is value determined in education, particularly with the existence of a monopolistic and bureaucratic public school system? In the rational choice paradigm, individuals, including school officials, pursue their own self-interests. In this framework, government bureaucrats determine what is valued in education based on their self-interest.

Concern about schools being dominated by the interests of educational bureaucrats was one reason Friedman proposed allowing parents to use a government voucher for educational expenses to choose any approved public or private school for their children. In his 1955 essay "The Role of Government in Education" and his 1962 book *Capitalism and Freedom*,[ii] he argued that a government subsidy for schools could be justified by "neighborhood effects," where a lack of schooling by one individual might have negative effects on others, such as unemployment and crime. But, Friedman argued, this justification did not require "nationalization" of education, by which he meant the "actual administration of educational institutions by government."[60] The combination of government subsidy and administration of schools results, he argued, in higher costs and lower quality education, particularly for the poor who reside in low-income school districts.

Consequently, Friedman advocated government subsidies to support educational choice between public, private, and for-profit schools.[61] In *Capitalism and Freedom*, he argued that vouchers would allow low-income families to choose schools of better quality than existed in public schools in low-income neighborhoods. Friedman proposed that government vouchers could be used to pay for an education at schools meeting minimum government standards. In explaining his proposed voucher system, Friedman argued that parents would able to determine the "value" of the educational services being provided.

> A major reason for this kind of use of public money is the present system of combining the administration of schools with their financing. The parent who would prefer to see money used for better teachers and texts rather than coaches and corridors has no way of expressing their preference except by persuading a majority to change the mixture for all. *This is a special case of the general principle that a market permits each to satisfy his own taste—effective proportional representation; whereas the political process imposes conformity* [author's emphasis].[62]

Important for Friedman's argument was that vouchers could be used at for-profit schools. Government vouchers for use at for-profit schools fit his model of an educational marketplace and provided lasting justification for for-profit schooling. Friedman explained it this way:

---

ii. Friedman's 1962 book *Capitalism and Freedom* contains the same arguments for school choice, in some cases almost word for word, as his 1955 essay. As I will explain, missing from the 1962 volume is Friedman's justification for Southerners to choose segregation academies after the 1954 Supreme Court decision making school segregation unconstitutional.

> Governments could require a minimum level of schooling financed by giving parents vouchers redeemable for a specified maximum sum per child per year if spent on "approved" educational services. Parents would then be free to spend this sum and any additional sum they themselves provided on purchasing educational services from an "approved" institution of their own choice. The educational services could be *rendered by private enterprises operated for profit, or by non-profit institutions* [author's emphasis].[63]

In the framework of economization, Friedman justified educational vouchers as creating a free market for goods and services in which parents could select an education for their children that they personally valued. Friedman's goal was for the marketplace and not bureaucrats to determine value or price of educational goods and services. He also claimed that competition in the marketplace would promote efficiency and thus reduce educational costs. These arguments all assume rational choice on the part of parents where they decide the benefits and costs of education provided by a particular school.

His 1955 essay on the role of government in education emphasized freedom of ideas as a justification for school choice. But, as I will explain, choice and freedom of ideas might have negative "neighborhood effects" particularly regarding racial attitudes. "Neighborhood effects" is Friedman's justification for government involvement in education. In his 1955 essay he stresses the teaching of "common social values required for a stable society."[64] However, he never specifies what these core values are. The closest he comes to identifying them is in the statement: "there is considerable agreement, approximating unanimity, on the appropriate content of an educational program for citizens of a democracy—the three R's cover the ground."[65] Under his school choice proposal, the government would subsidize parents to choose a public or private school that met government standards for teaching reading, writing, and arithmetic.

In 1955, Friedman encountered a significant problem for his choice proposal after the 1954 Supreme Court decision ending racial segregation of schools which resulted in the growth of private white academies.[66] In an almost full-page footnote in small font, Friedman wrote, "Essentially this proposal [school choice]—public financing but private operation of education—has recently been suggested in several southern states as a means of evading the Supreme Court ruling against segregation . . . My initial reaction—and I venture to predict, that of most readers—that this possible use of the proposal was a count against."[67] However, he discounted his initial reaction on the principle of free speech. While stating that he deplored segregation and racial prejudice, Friedman wrote, "it is not an appropriate function of the state to try to force individuals to act in accordance with my—anyone else's—views, whether about racial prejudice or the party to vote for."[68] He argued that as long as schools are publicly operated then he would choose forced nonsegregation over segregation.

Alluding to the existence of summer camps that were all Jewish, all Christian, and some of mixed religions, Friedman asked, "Is it an appropriate function of the state to prohibit the unmixed camps?"[69] He argued that one could propagate views that favored mixed camps while allowing for the existence of religiously segregated summer camps. In this framework, he argued the government could make funds available to parents to use "solely in segregated schools" or "solely in nonsegregated schools."[70] He concluded, "The proposed plan is not there-fore inconsistent with either forced segregation or forced nonsegregation. The point is that it makes available a third alternative."[71] The third alternative to requiring schools to be racially segregated or nonsegregated, as reflected in his discussion of summer camps, was giving parents the choice of racially segregated or racially mixed schools, while propagating views against racial segregation. In other words, he proposed that government subsidies would allow parents, either black or white, to choose a racially segregated school as long as the government did not require segregation.

Gary Becker, Milton Friedman's colleague at the University of Chicago and former student, echoed Friedman's call for education vouchers in his columns in *Business Week* that appeared from the late 1980s into the late 1990s. Becker would complain that public schools were making education too expensive: "The average public school . . . spends over $5,000 per student per year. Yet many parochial and other private schools provide better education with smaller expen-ditures . . . A generous voucher system could cost only half of what is spent by public schools."[72] In writing about a proposed voucher plan for California, Becker stated, "this competition [between public and private schools] for students would force public schools to become better."[73] Becker also echoed Friedman's argu-ment that vouchers would allow students to escape low-quality schools in low-income neighborhoods: "Disadvantaged families cannot afford private-school tuition and can seldom move to communities with better public schools. Usu-ally they must accept whatever public schools are available, no matter how bad. A voucher system would give these families some of the schooling alternatives now open only to middle-class and rich families."[74] Reflecting on the goal of his mentor to give parents an education that they valued, Becker wrote, "Some 30 years ago, Milton Friedman proposed a voucher system for schooling. Many critics considered his proposal wild and impractical . . . Education vouchers now seem rather tame compared with privatization of the postal system, prisons . . . A voucher system for education is an idea whose time has finally come."[75]

Theodore Schultz: The Economic Value of Education

Theodore Schultz's 1963 interpretative essay on the economic value of educa-tion relies on earlier works on educational economics. Reflecting the growing economization of education, Shultz wrote, "The economic value of educa-tion depends predominantly on the demand for and the supply of schooling approached as an investment."[76] Using the data on the costs of schooling, school attendance, and rates-of-return on investment in education, Schultz asserted that, "As a source of economic growth, the additional schooling of the labor force would *appear* to account for about one fifth of the growth in real national income in the United States between 1929 and 1957 [author's emphasis]."[77]

I emphasized the word "appear" in the above quote to indicate that Schultz did not provide any data that proved that additional schooling increased economic growth. He did provide data that the economy and schooling expanded at the same time during the first half of the twentieth century, but provided no proof of a causal relationship. In fact, and this is a problem in the work of other economists I am considering, he never discusses the economic, social and political changes that took place between 1929 and 1957. For instance, during the 1930s, unemployment of the depression years caused many youth to remain in school and during these years the high school became a mass institution. After WWII, fears of a postwar depression resulted in government funding of veterans to enter college. In addition, there was a postwar economic boom as compared to the lean years of the depression.[78] Also, the 1951 military draft with exemptions for college attendance prompted many men to go to college.[79] None of these events are considered by Schultz in his conclusion that education causes economic growth.

In 2009, economist Andrew Hacker challenged this conclusion by offering another possible interpretation. What about the possibility that education expanded because the economy grew in the early twentieth century rather than expansion of education causing economic growth? Hacker offered this alternative interpretation to highlight the questionable nature of human capital conclusions. He did not offer any proof for either interpretation of historic income and education data.[80]

In the early 1960s, Schultz claimed that economic interest in education was "laying the foundations for an economic growth policy which assigns a major role to schooling."[81] Schultz was correct about the future emphasis on education as a contributor to economic growth.

Schultz's reasoning that investment in education would reduce income inequality was supported by the free market ideas of the Chicago School. Schultz foreshadowed future policy by advancing the hypothesis that "changes in the investment in human capital are a basic factor reducing the inequality in the personal distribution of income."[82] He did not provide any proof to support this statement, but relied on data from studies of the first half of the century. Dismissing government actions to reduce income inequalities, he wrote, "changes in income transfers in progressive taxation, and changes in the distribution of privately owned wealth have been overrated as factors in altering the personal distribution of income."[83] Policies that could be derived from Schultz's book included investing in education for economic growth and reducing income inequalities, while cutting progressive and estate taxes.

Shultz also foreshadowed calls for skill-based schooling. The logical question after arguing that schooling caused economic growth and reduced income inequalities was: What did students learn in school that contributed to these economic results? Was it everything that students studied or particular subjects? Did the study of history advance the economy or was it math and science? As readers are probably aware, the future answer to these questions was that schools should focus on literacy, math, science, technology, and engineering. He wrote, much to the future chagrin of devotees of history, literature, and the arts, "the value of schooling will be enhanced by more precise knowledge of its contribution to *skills* and other capabilities which increase the earnings of human agents [author's emphasis]."[84]

His international perspective and background in the economics of agriculture were reflected in Shultz's 1970 Nobel Prize speech. The speech focused on the plight of the farming poor in India. To ease the poverty of India, Shultz recommended focusing on human capital. He said, "most observers overate the economic importance of land and greatly underrate the importance of the quality of human agents."[85] Essentially, Schultz was praising an era which saw increased use of fertilizers, pesticides, and, eventually, genetically modified crops. For Schultz it was the application of human knowledge to farming that would override what he called, "A widely held view—the natural earth view . . . that there is a virtually fixed land area suitable for growing food . . . According to this view, it is impossible to continue to produce enough food for the growing world population."[86] Reflecting a faith in human reason and science to solve environmental problems, Schultz told the gathered dignitaries, "An alternative view—the social-economic view—is that man has the ability and intelligence to lessen his dependence on cropland, on traditional agriculture and on depleting sources of energy and can reduce real costs of producing food for the growing world population."[87]

Schultz's speech reflected many different aspects of the Chicago School. First was a faith in the marketplace to find solutions for human problems through the work of entrepreneurs: "When governments have taken over this function [the marketplace] in farming, they prevented this entrepreneurial talent from being used."[88] In the twenty-first century, the World Economic Forum would call for the introduction of entrepreneurship education, as I discuss in Chapter 5, as a solution to global economic problems. Second, he stressed the importance of investing in human capital to drive economies and transform economic sectors such as farming. Influenced by Schultz, his colleague Gary Becker would push for an agenda of human capital development.

Gary Becker: Human Capital and Economization of the Family

A good example of the economization of education is Gary Becker's definition of a school as given in his famous and influential book *Human Capital*: "A school can be defined as an institution specializing in the production of training, as distinct from a firm that offers training in conjunction with the production of goods."[89] Using this definition of a school, Becker analyzed the relationship between education and income and came to the conclusion that personal investment in education resulted in a high rate-of-return. And, while somewhat smaller, the rates-of-return for public investment in education were significant. Becker's conclusions would affect education policies well into the twenty-first century and would become part of the standard rhetoric of global groups such as OECD, the World Economic Forum, and the World Bank, and were embedded in the education plans of many nations. For Becker and his followers, the goals of investment in education were increased personal income and general economic growth. An important result of economic growth was to be decreasing inequality of incomes. Later arguments would emphasize that investment in education was key to the economic development of poorer countries.

In *Human Capital*, Becker determined the investment value of education by comparing rates-of-return on investment in college or high school. His major focus was on college graduates and college dropouts with the actual cost of their college attendance being compared to lifetime economic benefits. In the framework of the rational choice paradigm a person chooses to invest money in a college education because they see economic benefits that are greater than the costs of attendance. Becker estimated the private rate-of-return for white male college graduates in 1939 to be 14.5 percent, while for white male college graduates in 1949 it was 12.7 percent.[90] What about college dropouts who invest in only a few years of post-secondary education? Becker estimated for urban, native whites, college dropouts were 8.2 to 11.6 percent in 1939 and in 1949 around 9.5 percent.[91] These rates-of-return, according to Becker, "exceed those on business capital."

What about nonwhites? In reporting these rates-of-return, Becker differentiated between Southern and Northern states. The rate-of-return on investment in college for Southern nonwhite males in 1939, he estimated, was between 10.6 to 14 percent, and for Northern nonwhites it was 8.3 to 12.3 percent.[92] As a result of these estimates and using the rational choice paradigm, Becker concluded, "This evidence indicates that nonwhite male high-school graduates have less incentive than white graduates, but not much less, to go to college."[93]

What about the role of "ability" in achieving high income? Becker defined ability as IQ scores, interest in schooling, perseverance, and knowledge about professional and managerial occupations.[94] Becker suggests a strong correlation between level of education and ability. However, according to his estimates, "The evidence suggests that this correlation [between ability and level of education] explains only a small part of the apparently large return [for college attendance]."[95] This would suggest that all people, even those with low abilities, will economically benefit from college attendance. In comparing the differences in earnings between high school and college graduates, Becker wrote: "By and large, it appears, ability explains only a relatively small part of the differentials and college education explains the larger part."[96]

Becker's conclusions regarding the effect of schooling on society resulted in later proposals to invest in education to increase economic growth. Becker recognized the difficulty of determining a rate-of-return from public investment in education, particularly in higher education. He estimated a range of possible rates-of-return. At the lower end of his estimates for public gains, Becker asserted, they "do not differ much from the private rates of return."[97] His upper estimate of rate-of-return was almost double. His conclusion was that the rate-of-return from investing in college was higher than business investments in capital.

Important for later arguments on the relationship between educational investments and economic growth is Becker's reliance on Edward Denison's 1962 study *The Sources of Economic Growth in the United States*.[98] Becker referred to Denison's work as "indirect and not [using a] very reliable method."[99] Denison estimated the contribution of physical capital, labor, and other factors to US economic growth. After subtracting their contribution growth, Denison labeled the residual "advancement in knowledge."[100] Denison then estimated that from 1929 to 1957 "advancement in knowledge" contributed .58 percent to income growth and growth in education contributed .67 percent. As a result of Denison's study and his own estimates, Becker concluded, "the estimated social rate on college education could be as much as twice and as little as less than half of that on business capital."[101] In other words, despite his hesitancy in using Denison's work, Becker was able to send out a message that resounded through the years that investment in human capital resulted in general economic benefits that more or less equaled that of other business investments.

The link between educational investments and economic growth received a central place in Becker's coauthored essay with Kevin M. Murphy and Robert Tamara that was added to the 1993 edition of *Human Capital*. The essay stated what would become the mantra of human capital economists: "Yet the evidence is now quite strong of a close link between investments in human capital and growth. Since human capital is embodied knowledge and skills, and economic development depends on advances in technological and scientific knowledge, development presumably depends on the accumulation human capital."[102]

The above statement was supported with references to Theodore Schultz's 1960 essay "Capital Formation in Education" which estimated that between 1910 and 1950 investment in education grew more rapidly than investment in physical capital. By themselves, these figures do not prove that education contributed to economic growth. In fact, the change in investments over this period might be attributable to the depression years when government policies tried to persuade unemployed youth to leave the labor market and return to high schools and colleges.[103] Becker supports Schultz's findings by citing Edward Denison that the growth in years of schooling "explained" about 25 percent of US per capita income between 1929 and 1982. Becker then cites findings that, after 1960,

100 countries reported that investment in education increased national income. Becker used the word "suggest" in reporting these international findings.[104] The words "explain" and "suggest" give a tentative quality to these findings.

Another lasting contribution of Becker's work was linking expanded educational opportunities to decreasing differences in income or, in other words, reducing income inequalities. After 1980, when as I will explain, income inequalities increased, there would continue a belief among some that education would be key to closing the income gap.

In *Human Capital*, Becker argued that income inequalities would be reduced as uniform investment decisions by all businesses would increase all wages by the same proportion along with wage differences. However, he argued within the framework of the rational choice paradigm, wage differentials would create an incentive to invest in human capital increasing the supply of skilled persons. "The increased supply would in turn reduce the rate of increase of wage differences and produce an *absolute narrowing of wage ratios* [author's emphasis]."[105]

The reader will recall that economist Herbert Simon criticized Becker for just this type of application of the rational choice paradigm without any supporting evidence. There is no actual evidence that wage differences declined because of rational decisions to invest in education. Becker's argument is pure speculation based simply on findings that wage differences did decrease as educational investments increased during the early twentieth century. Simon could contend that Becker's argument lacks analysis of the impact of WWI, the depression, and WWII on US culture and the economy. For the same reason, Simon might criticize Becker's argument that investment in education contributes to economic growth based on studies that just analyze income data from the 1920s to the 1980s while neglecting the profound social, political, and cultural changes during the period.

Becker's lack of proof for his assertions, while relying on the rational choice paradigm, would, in the twenty-first century, erupt in criticisms of claims that investment in education and economic growth reduces income inequalities. In fact, income inequalities have globally increased, as I will explain, from the 1980s to the present despite more money invested in schools and economic growth.

Do Educational Investments Reduce Income Inequalities?

The rush to conclusions and the myopic view of some economists can be found in the debate about growing inequality of incomes. The issue centers on Simon Kuznets' analysis of US income data from 1913 to 1948. Kuznets worked with Milton Friedman at the National Bureau of Economic research prior to Friedman taking a position at the University of Chicago.[106] Kuznets' pioneering work on US national income used federal income tax from its inception in 1913. One of the things the income tax data showed was that inequalities in income were reduced from 1913 to 1948. Why?[107]

Income data by itself does not provide an explanation for the decrease in income inequalities. Kuznets provides no evidence of a causal relationship. However, in his 1954 presidential address to the American Economic Association, later published as "Economic Growth and Income Inequality," Kuznets interpreted the data as showing the income inequality would decrease as larger parts of the population experienced economic growth. Referred to as Kuznets' curve, he argued that income inequalities followed a bell curve rising during the early part of industrialization and then declining rapidly. Kuznets' income data from 1913 to 1948 seemed to support this conclusion.[108]

However, from the 1970s to the present, US income inequality has actually increased so that inequality, according to one report, was greater in 2010 than it had been in 1913.[109] The Pew Research Center claimed, "U.S. income inequality has been increasing steadily since the 1970s, and now has reached levels not seen since 1928."[110] What happened to Kuznets' curve and the promise of greater income equality? French economist Thomas Piketty argues that Kuznets' curve was simplistic and ignored the broad panorama of economic events and global upheavals from 1913 to 1948. Piketty writes, "The sharp reduction in income inequality that we observe in almost all rich countries between 1914 and 1945 was due above all to the world wars and the violent economic and political shocks they entailed (especially for people with large fortunes)."[111]

As Piketty noted, Kuznets' curve served political interests, particularly those supporting government policies favoring business. Along with those supporting free market ideas, those accepting Kuznets' optimistic vision supported government deregulation of business controls and reducing corporate and personal taxes. It could be considered support for a trickledown theory of economics, where one didn't have to worry about government policies favoring business and the rich because all would supposedly benefit as economic growth reduced the gap between the rich and poor. Kuznets' curve also presents a rosy picture of the future of economic growth in developing countries, where a small group might initially receive the majority of economic benefits with the promise that all would eventually benefit and the initial large income inequalities would disappear.

The Rhetoric of Education Investments and Global Economic Growth

The questionable assertions of a causal relationship between education and economic growth began to appear in the rhetoric of global institutions. As I will detail in later chapters, OECD, the World Bank, and the World Economic Forum, along with national education leaders, began to unquestioningly claim that education would be the panacea for economic growth and development, poverty, unemployment, and income inequalities. This argument eventually led to calls for education to focus on teaching skills needed by global businesses.

From an economization perspective, schools were to function as appendages to the global economic system.

In this chapter, I will use two examples, more will appear in later chapters, to illustrate how these economic assumptions became part of education rhetoric. One is the early goal of the World Bank to fund education in developing countries to spur economic growth. When Robert McNamara became head of the World Bank in 1968, he echoed the work of Becker and Schultz, "Our aim here will be to provide assistance where it will contribute most to *economic development. This will mean emphasis on educational planning, the starting point for the whole process of educational improvement* [author's emphasis]."[112]

The second example is taken from the 1983 US report *A Nation at Risk; The Imperative of Education Reform* released by the US National Commission on Excellence in Education. The report was written as the US and other economies were slowly emerging from a period of high unemployment and inflation or, as it was called, stagflation.[113] The report, using the rhetoric of human capital, blamed the economic woes on poor schooling.

In other words, *A Nation at Risk* turned the whole argument on education and the economy on its head by claiming that failure of schools caused failures in national and global economies. The report opens with the startling words, "Our Nation is at risk. Our once unchallenged preeminence in commerce, industry, science, and technological innovation is being overtaken by competitors throughout the world . . . If an unfriendly foreign power had attempted to impose on America the mediocre educational performance that exists today, we might well have viewed it as an act of war."[114]

The report marshaled no evidence that the supposed decline in educational quality actually caused an economic decline. Nothing is cited in the report about the time it takes for a school graduate to impact the economy. For instance: Do graduates entering the workforce immediately bring down the economy or does it take time? What period of schooling is the report referring to with its claims of economic disaster? Were they graduates of the 1950s who would have been somewhere in their thirties and forties in the 1980s? Or were they graduates of the 1970s?

There was nothing in the report that proved a causal relationship between a supposed decline in educational quality and an economic decline. The report cites test scores and other education data to prove a decline in the quality of US students. Some of this data is questionable because it shows no relationship between test scores and a declining US economy in the 1970s and 1980s. For instance, the report gives as evidence: "Average achievement of high school students on most standardized tests is now lower than 26 years ago when Sputnik was launched."[115] Certainly, student test scores in the late 1970s or 1980s were not immediately bringing down the economy of the 1980s since these students had either just entered the workforce or were still in school. If they had just entered the workforce it is doubtful they had an immediate impact.

Also, the report took the reasoning of human capital economist a step further by claiming that low-quality schooling was reducing the ability of the US to compete in the global economy:

> The risk is not only that the Japanese make automobiles more efficiently than Americans and have government subsidies for development and export. It is not just that the South Koreans recently built the world's most efficient steel mill, or that American machine tools, once the pride of the world, are being displaced by German products. It is also that these developments signify a redistribution of trained capability throughout the globe. Knowledge, learning, information, and skilled intelligence are the new raw materials of international commerce and are today spreading throughout the world as vigorously as miracle drugs, synthetic fertilizers, and blue jeans did earlier. If only to keep and improve on the slim competitive edge we still retain in world markets, we must dedicate ourselves to the reform of our educational system for the benefit of all—old and young alike, affluent and poor, majority and minority. Learning is the indispensable investment required for success in the "information age" we are entering.[116]

A Nation at Risk, like McNamara at the World Bank, placed the questionable conclusions derived from historical US income data into a global economic context. The statement that poor-quality education was causing the US economy to fall behind that of Japan, South Korea, and Germany was made without any proof of a causal relationship. Like Kuznets, Shultz, and Becker, the report ignores changes in global political, social, and economic conditions, which in this case, involves a whole host of factors after WWII, such as, to only name a few, the breakup of colonial empires, the reconstruction of the postwar economies of Japan and Germany, global migration, changes in international finance, and the growth of multinational corporations.

The Economization of Life

Gary Becker's *Business Week* columns along with his book on the family reflect the increasing application of economic methods, particularly the rational choice paradigm, to all aspects of life. As I discuss in Chapter 6, the application of the rational choice paradigm to the family led to a portrait of the ideal family for global corporations and a global call for preschool education to solve the problems of poverty. I will discuss Becker's *A Treatise on the Family* in more detail in Chapter 6 along with the work of another member of the Chicago School and Nobel Prize winner James Heckman and his economic analysis of preschool and family life.

For instance, consider Becker's application of rational choice and free market theories to crime which supported harsher and mandatory sentences which supported policies that grew the prison population and the privatization of prisons. In a 1985 *Business Week* column, "The Economic Approach to Fighting Crime," Becker wrote, "in recent decades more persons were induced to commit crimes, or commit additional crimes, because crime became a more attractive 'occupation' when punishment became less certain and less severe."[117] From the standpoint of the rational choice paradigm, the potential criminal makes a calculation as to whether or not the benefits of the crime outweigh the potential punishment. Of course, this narrow economic approach to the causes of crime discounts any possible social causes. Consequently Becker argues, "crimes of passion as well as crimes against property are reduced by making punishment more certain and more severe."

More severe punishments result in more prisoners with longer sentences. Public institutions such as prisons, according to Becker, could operate more efficiently and at lower costs if they were privatized. In a 1986 column "Why Public Enterprises Belong in Private Hands," Becker argued that political and labor union influences often forced public enterprises to make uneconomical decisions. Referring to privatization efforts in the 1980s by President Ronald Reagan and British Prime Minister Margaret Thatcher, Becker wrote, "The sale of government enterprises to the private sector can—and should—be carried much further. Publicly owned enterprises apparently are less efficient and less flexible than competitive private companies because they are unable to separate economic choices from political considerations."[118]

I am not claiming that Becker or the rational choice paradigm were responsible for the increasing US prison population after the 1980s. I am only stating that this economic reasoning supported the trend. Beginning in the 1980s, the US prison population increased from less than 400,000 inmates to 1,570,400 in 2012 after a small decline from 2010. In 2012/2013, the US topped international rates of incarceration with 716 out of 100,000 people in prison. This rate was followed by Rwanda with 492 per 100,000 in prison. A striking contrast is that Sweden has an incarceration rate of 67 per 100,000.[119] In 2011, 8 percent of US prisoners were in privatized prisons.[120]

Conclusion: The Economic Value of Education

In the next chapter, I discuss the "skills gap" as portrayed by major global institutions and global businesses. As mentioned previously, economists like Theodore Schultz wanted to identify the specific skills learned in college that contribute to income growth. Inevitably, as I discuss in the next chapter, this did occur for all levels of schooling and would lead to questions like: What skills can be learned in philosophy and history that will contribute to growth in personal income and the general economy?

Reflecting the continuing economization of education, the *New York Times* reported in 2014 that the US Department of Education was continuing to develop a college rating system that "would compare schools on factors like how many of their students graduate, *how much debt their students accumulate and how much money their students earn after graduating* [author's emphasis]."[121] This rating system adopts the investment rhetoric initiated by the Chicago School in the 1950s and 1960s by comparing college debt to income after graduation. College presidents reacted to the proposed rating system by saying it would "elevate financial concerns above academic ones and would punish schools with liberal arts programs and large numbers of students who major in programs like theater arts, social work or education, disciplines that do not typically lead to lucrative jobs."[122]

Will the economization of education lead to the death of liberal arts or force these courses to teach job skills? Victor E. Ferrall Jr., President Emeritus of Beloit College and author of Liberal Arts at the Brink, said, reflecting the reality of the economization of educational thinking, "the number of Americans who see the great value a liberal arts education provides is dwindling . . . In today's market, how is anyone going to get a job as an anthropologist or historian, let alone as a philosopher or expert in 19th-century English literature?"[123]

Liberal arts colleges have responded to economization trends by changing course content so that they can be considered vocational. Ferrall asserts, "An increasing number of liberal arts colleges are attempting to answer this question by presenting themselves as vocational, or by arguing that studying anthropology will actually lead to a good job."[124] He recommended that liberal arts education should be presented as teaching skills needed for employment, such as "questioning, analytic, critical thinking that stands recipients in good stead wherever their lives may lead and on whatever career paths they follow."[125]

As schools shift to skills-based curricula the rhetoric of rates-of-return on educational investments continue as student loans result, in 2014, in debts of over $1 trillion. Saddled with debt, students might wonder if college was a good investment. According to MIT economist David Autor, "four-year college degrees made 98 percent more an hour on average in 2013 than people without a degree. That's up from 89 percent five years earlier, 85 percent a decade earlier and 64 percent in the early 1980s."[126] After considering the cost of tuition and fees, Autor calculated that the amount of lifetime returns on investment in college as compared to the lifetime income of high school graduates was $500,000.

The triumph of the economization of education is highlighted by liberal arts becoming vocational; evaluation and rankings based on rates-of-return for educational investment; and shaping college, preschool, primary, middle, and secondary courses to teach skills for the workplace.

Notes

1 Gary Becker, "The Economic Way of Looking at Life," (Nobel Prize Lecture, December 9, 1992). Retrieved from Nobelprize.org, "The Official Web Site of the Nobel Prize," http://www.nobelprize.org/nobel_prizes/economic-sciences/laureates/1992/becker-lecture.html on May 7, 2014.

2 Gary Becker, *Human Capital: A Theoretical and Empirical Analysis with Special Reference to Education* Third Edition (Chicago: The University of Chicago Press, 1993). Because of its popularity *Human Capital* was reissued after its 1964 publication in two other editions in 1975 and 1993. Each new edition contained a new introduction.

3 See Johan Van Overtveldt, *The Chicago School: How the University of Chicago Assembled the Thinkers Who Revolutionized Economics and Business* (Chicago: Agate Publishing, 2007).

4 Gary Becker and Guity Nashat Becker, *The Economics of Life: From Baseball to Affirmative Action to Immigration, How Real-World Issues Affect Our Everyday Life* (New York: McGraw-Hill, 1997).

5 Milton Friedman, "The Role of Government in Education" in *Economics and the Public Interest* edited by Robert A. Solo (New Brunswick: Rutgers University Press, 1955), pp. 123–144 and Milton Friedman, *Capitalism and Freedom* (Chicago: The University of Chicago Press, 2002), p. 88. The University of Chicago published three editions of the book in 1962, 1982, and 2002.

6 Gary Becker, "Milton Friedman" in *Remembering The University of Chicago: Teachers, Scientists, and Scholars* edited by Edward Shils (Chicago: University of Chicago, 1991), p. 142.

7 Friedman, *Capitalism and Freedom* . . . , p. 88.

8 Ibid., p. 88.

9 Ibid., p. 89.

10 Ibid., p. 100.

11 Milton and Rose Friedman, *Free to Choose: A Personal Statement* (New York: Harcourt Inc., 1990), p. 157.

12 Ibid., p. 157.

13 Ibid., p. 176.

14 Ibid., p. 177.

15 Ibid., p. 179.

16 Ibid., p. 179.

17 Theodore Schultz, *The Economic Value of Education* (New York: Columbia University Press, 1963).

18 Ibid., pp. 12–13.

19 Ibid., p. 7.

20 Gary Becker, *Human Capital* . . . , p. 29.

21 Kok-Yee Ng, Mei Ling Tan, and Soon Ang, "Global Cultural Capital and Cosmopolitan Human Capital: The Effects of Global Mindset and Organizational Routines on Cultural Intelligence and International Experience" in *The Oxford Handbook of Human Capital* edited by Alan Burton-Jones and J. C. Spender (Oxford: Oxford University Press, 2011), p. 75.

22 Alan Burton-Jones and J. C. Spender, "Concept and Rationale: Why a Handbook of Human Capital?" in *The Oxford Handbook of Human Capital* . . . , pp. 1–2.

23 Universal Military Training and Service Act of 1951—Hearings before the Preparedness Subcommittee of the Committee on Armed Forces, United States Senate, Eighty Second Congress, First Session, January 10–February 2 (Washington, DC: Government Printing Office, 1951), pp. 53–54.

24 Dwight Eisenhower, "Our Future Security," reprinted in *Science and Education for National Defense: Hearings before the Committee on Labor and Public Welfare, United States Senate, Eighty-fifth Congress, Second Session* (Washington, DC: Government Printing Office, 1958), p. 1360.

25 See Joel Spring, *The Sorting Machine Revisited: National Educational Policy Since 1945* Updated Edition (White Plains, NY: Longman, 1989), pp. 63–93.
26 Craufurd D. Goodwin, "The Patrons of Economics in a Time of Transformation" in *From Interwar Pluralism to Postwar Neoclassicism* edited by Mary S. Morgan and Malcolm Rutherford (Durham, NC: Duke University Press, 1998), p. 54.
27 Mary S. Morgan and Malcolm Rutherford, "American Economics: The Character of the Transformation" in *From Interwar Pluralism to Postwar Neoclassicism . . .* , p. 16.
28 See Spring, *The Sorting Machine Revisited . . .* , pp. 1–24.
29 "The Problem of Poverty in America," *The Annual Report of the Council of Economic Advisers* (Washington, DC: Government Printing Office, 1964), p. 56.
30 As quoted in Brian Keeley, *Human Capital: How What You Know Shapes Your Life* (Paris: OECD Publishing, 2007), p. 29.
31 Becker, *Human Capital . . .* , pp. 29–160.
32 Margaret M. Blair, "An Economic Perspective on the Notion of 'Human Capital'" in *The Oxford Handbook of Human Capital* edited by Alan Burton-Jones and J.C. Spender (Oxford: Oxford University Press, 2011), p. 51.
33 Patrick Flanery, *Fallen Land* (New York: Riverhead Books, 2013), p. 142.
34 Ibid., p. 304.
35 Ibid., p. 141.
36 Ibid., pp. 210–226.
37 Ibid., p. 42.
38 Bradley W. Bateman, "Clearing the Ground: The Demise of the Social Gospel Movement and the Rise of Neoclassicism in American Economics" in *From Interwar Pluralism to Postwar Neoclassicism . . .* , pp. 29–52.
39 Goodwin, "The Patrons of Economics in a Time of Transformation . . .," p. 59.
40 Ibid., p. 59.
41 Gary Becker, *A Treatise on the Family* (Cambridge: Harvard University Press, 1993). There were three editions of this book published in 1981, 1991, and 1993.
42 Ibid., p. 191.
43 Ibid., p. 192.
44 Robin M. Hogarth and Melvin W. Reder, eds., *Rational Choice: The Contrast between Economics and Psychology* (Chicago: University of Chicago Press, 1986).
45 Robin M. Hogarth and Melvin W. Reder, "Introduction: Perspectives from Economics and Psychology" in *Rational Choice . . .* , pp. 1–24.
46 Ibid., p. 21.
47 Herbert A. Simon, "Rationality in Psychology and Economics" in Hogarth and Reder, eds., *Rational Choice . . .* , pp. 29–30.
48 Ibid., p. 30. The original quote can be found in Becker, *A Treatise on the Family . . .* , p. 350.
49 Becker, *A Treatise on the Family . . .* , pp. 354–355.
50 Simon, "Rationality in Psychology and Economics" . . . , p. 31.
51 Overtveldt, *The Chicago School . . .* , pp. 75–76.
52 Friedman, *Capitalism and Freedom . . .* , pp. 100–101.
53 Ibid., p. 103.
54 See Spring, *The Sorting Machine Revisited . . .* , pp. 93–123.
55 Mont Pelerin Society, "About MPS." Retrieved from https://www.montpelerin.org/montpelerin/mpsAbout.html on May 14, 2014.
56 Ibid.
57 Overtveldt, *The Chicago School . . .* , p. 343.

58 Ibid., pp. 343–344.

59 Friedrich Hayek, *The Road to Serfdom* (Chicago: University of Chicago Press, 1994).

60 Friedman, "The Role of Government in Education . . . ," pp. 125–130 and *Capitalism and Freedom* . . . , pp. 86–88.

61 Friedman, "The Role of Government in Education . . . ," p. 144 and *Capitalism and Freedom* . . . , p. 89.

62 *Capitalism and Freedom* . . . , p. 94.

63 Ibid., p. 89.

64 Friedman, "The Role of Government in Education . . . ," pp. 128–129.

65 Ibid., p. 133.

66 For a discussion of this decision see Joel Spring, *The American School: A Global Context from the Puritans to the Obama Administration*, Ninth Edition (New York: McGraw-Hill, 2011), pp. 386–401.

67 Friedman, "The Role of Government in Education . . . ," p. 131.

68 Ibid., p. 131.

69 Ibid., p. 131.

70 Ibid., p. 131.

71 Ibid., p. 131.

72 Becker and Becker, *The Economics of Life* . . . , p. 85.

73 Ibid., p. 83.

74 Ibid., p. 90.

75 Ibid., p. 91.

76 Schultz, *The Economic Value of Education* . . . , p. xi.

77 Ibid., p. 11.

78 Spring, *The American School* . . . , pp. 307–316.

79 Spring, *The Sorting Machine Revisited* . . . , pp. 40–53.

80 Andrew Hacker, "Where Will We Find the Jobs?" *The New York Review of Books* (February 24, 2011).

81 Schultz, *The Economic Value of Education* . . . , p. 19.

82 Ibid., p. 65.

83 Ibid., p. 62.

84 Ibid., *p. 51.*

85 Theodore Schultz, "The Economics of Being Poor," Lecture in memory of Alfred Nobel, December 8, 1979 retrieved from http://www.nobelprize.org/nobel_prizes/economic-sciences/laureates/1979/schultz-lecture.html on May 21, 2014, p. 1.

86 Ibid., p. 5.

87 Ibid., p. 5.

88 Ibid., p. 5.

89 Becker, *Human Capital* . . . , p. 51.

90 Ibid., pp. 168–171.

91 Ibid., pp. 184–185.

92 Ibid., p. 186.

93 Ibid., p. 186.

94 Ibid., pp. 171–172.

95 Ibid., p. 173.

96 Ibid., p. 247.

97 Ibid., p. 247.

98 Edward Denison, Sources of Economic Growth in the United States (Washington, DC: Committee for Economic Development, 1962).

99 Becker, *Human Capital* . . . , p. 210.

100 Ibid., p. 210.

101 Ibid., p. 212.

102 Gary Becker, Kevin M. Murphy, and Robert Tamara, "Human Capital, Fertility, and Economic Growth" in Becker, *Human Capital . . .* , p. 324.

103 Theodore Schultz, "Capital Formation by Education," *Journal of Political Economy* (December 1960), pp. 571–583.

104 Ibid., p. 324.

105 Becker, *Human Capital . . .* , p. 90

106 Overtveldt, *The Chicago School . . .* , p. 93.

107 I am relying for this account on the recent work by French economist Thomas Piketty in his *Capital in the Twenty-First Century* translated by Arthur Goldhammer (The Belknap Press of Harvard University Press, 2014).

108 Ibid., pp. 13–14.

109 Ibid., p. 324.

110 Drew DeSilver, "U.S. income inequality, on rise for decades, is now highest since 1928," (December 5, 2013). Retrieved from http://www.pewresearch.org/fact-tank/2013/12/05/u-s-income-inequality-on-rise-for-decades-is-now-highest-since-1928/ on May 25, 2014.

111 Ibid., p. 15.

112 Michael Goldman, *Imperial Nature: The World Bank and Struggles for Social Justice* (New Haven, CT: Yale University Press, 2005), p. 69.

113 See the description of this period in Piketty, *Capital in the Twenty-First Century . . .* , pp. 131–139.

114 National Commission on Excellence in Education, *A Nation at Risk; The Imperative of Education Reform* (Washington, DC: U.S. Government Printing Office, 1983), p. 9.

115 Ibid., p. 11.

116 Ibid., p. 10.

117 Gary Becker, "The Economic Approach to Fighting Crime" in The Economics of Life . . . , p. 143.

118 Gary Becker, "Why Public Enterprises Belong in Private Hands" in The Economics of Life . . . , p. 33.

119 The Sentencing Project, "Fact Sheet: Trends in U.S. Corrections." Retrieved from http://sentencingproject.org/doc/publications/inc_Trends_in_Corrections_Fact_sheet.pdf on May 22, 2014.

120 Cody Mason, "International Growth Trends in Prison Privatization (August 2013)," The Sentencing Project. Retrieved from http://sentencingproject.org/doc/publica-tions/inc_International%20Growth%20Trends%20in%20Prison%20Privatization.pdf on May 22, 2014.

121 Michael D. Shear, "Colleges Rattled as Obama Seeks Rating System." *New York Times* (May 25, 2014). Retrieved from http://www.nytimes.com/2014/05/26/us/colleges-rattled-as-obama-presses-rating-system.html?emc=eta1 on May 29, 2014.

122 Ibid.

123 Scott Jaschik, "Disappearing Liberal Arts Colleges," *Inside Higher Ed* (October 11, 2012). Retrieved from http://www.insidehighered.com/news/2012/10/11/study-finds-liberal-arts-colleges-are-disappearing#sthash.eWkF7ftc.dpbs on May 29, 2014.

124 Ibid.

125 Ibid.

126 David Leonhardt, "Is College Worth It? Clearly, New Data Say," *New York Times* (May 27, 2014). Retrieved from http://www.nytimes.com/2014/05/27/upshot/is-college-worth-it-clearly-new-data-say.html?emc=eta1&_r=0 on May 29, 2014.

2

OECD

The Economization of Test Scores

"The gains in test scores over time are strongly related to [economic] gains over time," argue economists Eric A. Hanushek and Ludger Woessman, and political scientist Paul E. Peterson in an updated 2013 version of human capital.[1] Test scores! How did test scores become a gauge of economic health? I use the term "updated" because this human capital argument highlights "test scores" in contrast to earlier discussions of the contribution of years of schooling and educational credentials to economic growth and productivity. The test scores referred to by the authors are from the OECD's Programme for International Student Assessment (PISA) and the International Association for the Evaluation of Educational Achievement (IEA)'s Trends in International Mathematics and Science Study (TIMSS).

OECD is responsible for making test scores a gauge of the quality of human capital and national economies. During the second half of the twentieth century, OECD played a major role in disseminating the ideas of the Chicago School of Economics, particularly Gary Becker and Theodore Shultz's link between education, human capital, and economic growth.

Called the "World Ministry of Education,"[2] OECD was a 1960 transformation of the Organization of European Economic Cooperation (OEEC) which was created in 1948 with American aid of $12 billion.[3] OEEC's goal was the economic reconstruction of Europe after WWII and, from the American perspective, blocking the expansion of Soviet influence.

OECD's original membership of 20 nations has expanded to 34 of the richest nations of the world. In addition, OECD provides expertise and exchanges ideas with more than 100 other countries including the least developed countries in Africa. In 2013, OECD offered this description of its activities:

The OECD provides a forum in which governments can work together to share experiences and seek solutions to common problems. We work with governments to understand what drives economic, social and environmental change. We measure productivity and global flows of trade and investment. We analyze and compare data to predict future trends. We set international standards on a wide range of things, from agriculture and tax to the safety of chemicals.[4]

OECD describes its educational work: "We compare how different countries' school systems are readying their young people for modern life."[5]

OECD, with its many publications and global testing programs, offers panaceas for the global economy. The organization's publications are infused with claims of saving humanity: "Together, our goal continues to be to build a stronger, cleaner, fairer world."[6] Emphasizing general humanitarian goals, the organization declares: "The mission of the Organization for Economic Co-operation and Development (OECD) is to promote policies that will improve the economic and social well-being of people around the world."[7] Membership is described as:

> Today, our 34 member countries span the globe, from North and South America to Europe and the Asia-Pacific region. They include *many of the world's most advanced countries* but also *emerging countries* like Mexico, Chile and Turkey. We also work closely with *emerging giants* like China, India and Brazil and developing economies in Africa, Asia, Latin America and the Caribbean.[8]

In 1995, IEA worked with OECD to collect data for the Third TIMSS. IEA officials called 1995 TIMSS "the largest and most ambitious study of comparative education undertaken."[9] In 1997 OECD launched PISA and its test scores quickly became part of an international academic Olympiad with nations competing for top results. OECD asserts that, PISA is in response to "member countries' demands for regular and reliable data on the knowledge and skills of their students and the performance of their education systems."[10] When PISA first began, OECD claimed: "PISA benefits from its worldwide scope and its regularity. More than 70 countries and economies have taken part in PISA so far and the surveys, which are given every three years, allow them to track their progress in meeting key learning goals."[11]

Is there a causal relation between scores on PISA and TIMSS and economic growth? Hanushek, Woessman, and Peterson, in equating the quality of human capital and cognitive skills with test scores, conclude, "a variety of tests support the claim that level of human capital acquired by young people while in school has a direct, causal effect on a country's economic growth rate. Further, these tests (PISA and TIMSS) indicate that school policy, if effective in raising cognitive skills, is an important force in economic development."[12]

How did ideas of human capital become global and measured by test scores? Partly, the answer is in the work of OECD. I will begin by describing OECD's role in globalizing concepts of human capital which originated in the "manpower"[i] policies of OECD's precursor, the OEEC. I will then detail OECD's role in the global economization of education and then turn to the issue of measuring human capital through an international testing program.

The Cold War and the OECD's Economization of Education

The Cold War influenced the work of the Chicago School of Economics, OEEC and OECD. With its emphasis on free market economics, the Chicago School of Economics received recognition as an antidote to the Soviet Union's brand of communism. During the 1950s, the OEEC adopted changes in American education designed to educate more scientists, engineers, and mathematicians to help in the arms race with the Soviet Union.[13] These Cold War manpower policies received considerable attention after the 1957 Soviet launching of the space satellite Sputnik. It appeared to many Americans and Europeans that the Soviet Union was achieving technological superiority because it was educating more and superior scientists and technical workers.[14]

OEEC was established in 1948 to help distribute American aid to European countries.[15] As part of a Cold War strategy, OEEC included a propaganda unit, "Information Program," which is described as "the largest international propaganda operation ever seen in peacetime."[16] These propaganda units were established in each of the OEEC countries issuing documentary films, broadcasting radio programs, and distributing millions of copies of pamphlets promoting American economic ideas. One exhibit explained, high productivity had "given the United States a high standard of living . . . increased per man output . . . [resulting in] betterment of living conditions, social progress, strength and ability to defend democratic institutions."[17] Summarizing this propaganda work, economist Graham Hutton wrote, "Higher productivity is the brightest hope for every man, woman and child that the standard of living can be maintained and improved."[18]

Foreshadowing the dominant human capital arguments of OECD, the OEEC in the 1950s shared US concerns with educating scientific and technical manpower (a term used in the 1950s). In 1958 the organization created the Office for Scientific and Technical Personnel. Increased productivity was to be accomplished through increasing the supply of scientific and technical personnel.[19]

---

i "Manpower," a term which currently might be considered sexist, was used in the 1950s and 1960s to describe the availability of educated workers for positions considered important for national defense and the economy.

The US focused on manpower planning after WWII by creating the National Science Foundation (1950), establishing a military draft that exempted those attending college (1951), and the National Manpower Council (1951).[20] Concerns about educating more scientific and technical personnel increased with the 1957 Sputnik launch which resulted in the 1958 National Defense Education Act promoting scientific and mathematical education. The hope was that the National Defense Education Act would increase the number of scientific, math, and engineering students to counter the technological advances of the Soviet Union. These changes were accompanied by the introduction in schools of new science and math curricula.[21]

The OEEC's Office for Scientific and Technical Personnel adopted many of the strategies implemented in the US to increase the number of scientists and technical workers for the purpose of increasing economic growth and productivity. There was even an attempt to introduce the new math and science curricula being introduced in US schools. Most importantly for the future work of OECD, the Office for Scientific and Technical Personnel began to engage in forecasting the future supply of educated workers at its 1959 Conference on Techniques for Forecasting Future Requirements of Scientific and Technical Personnel. The conference led to the 1960 publication of *Forecasting Manpower Needs for the Age of Science*.[22] This publication set the stage for later OECD national surveys of educational systems. At the time, the publication highlighted superiority of the US education system to that of European systems: "in 1959, 65 percent of an age group qualified for admission to higher education in the United States and Canada, the European percentage was 7 percent."[23]

The 1960 signing of the Convention on the Organization for Economic Cooperation and Development transformed OEEC into OECD. Concerns with scientific and technical manpower were now thought of in the framework of human capital economics. Reflecting the influence of American human capital economists, OECD in 1961 during its first year of operation held a conference in Washington, DC on "Economic Growth and Investment in Education."[24] In the same year, OECD established The Study Group in the Economics of Education.[25] OECD became committed to the economization of education.

As a major superpower emerging from WWII, the US dominated the activities of OEEC and, during its early years, OECD. Until the founding of OECD, US's primary Cold War strategy was countering Soviet military might with expanded defense spending and promoting global economic doctrines favorable to the US. OECD's emphasis on economic goals reflected a change in US Cold War strategy. US and OECD officials believed that increasing economic growth and productivity in Europe would deter Soviet influence and that of other leftist movements.[26]

The importance given by the OEEC to economists and manpower planning continued in OECD. A problem encountered in *Forecasting Manpower Needs for the Age of Science* was the lack of international standards for judging the quality and operation of national schools systems. OEEC set the stage for national education planning in the framework of employment needs and the quest to measure the output of national school systems.

OECD: The Triumph of Economization of Education

In a 2011 editorial commemorating 50 years of OECD work, Angel Gurría, OECD Secretary-General wrote, "At the new organization's Policy Conference on Economic Growth and Investment in Education, held in Washington, DC in 1961, emerging theories of human capital then being developed by Gary Becker, Theodore Schultz and others were brought center-stage in the international dialogue."[27] For a number of reasons, including the US's desire to expand membership in the organization and focus on economics, OECD expanded its geographical membership, making Canada and the United States members—they had been associates of OEEC—and adding Japan in 1964.[28]

The organization's 1960 founding Convention document highlights its emphasis on economics: "CONSIDERING that economic strength and prosperity are essential for the attainment of the purposes of the United Nations, the preservation of individual liberty and the increase of general well-being."[29] Article 2 of the Convention would eventually be translated into human capital goals; invest in education to grow the economy. Article 2 gives as organizational goals:

(a) promote the efficient use of their economic resources;
(b) in the scientific and technological field, promote the development of their resources, encourage research and promote vocational training;
(c) pursue policies designed to achieve economic growth and internal and external financial stability and to avoid developments which might endanger their economies or those of other countries.[30]

OECD's 1961 Washington DC Policy Conference on Economic Growth and Investment in Education addressed two questions:

1. The nature and the magnitude of the task facing education in the next decade to meet the needs of *social and economic progress* in the OECD area;
2. What should OECD countries do to respond effectively to the requests of the underdeveloped countries whose needs for educational expansion were relatively even greater than their own?[31]

The *Policy Conference on Economic Growth and Investment in Education Washington 16th–20th October 1961: Targets for Education in Europe in 1970* concluded that education planning should be founded "on the basic belief and assumption that more and better education for more people is desirable in itself and is at the same time *one of the most important factors in economic growth* [author's emphasis]."[32]

The human capital agenda was pushed to the forefront in Resolution 9 at the third meeting of the Conference on Economic Growth and Investment in Education in 1962: "Considering that expenditure on education is not only designed for the functioning of public service, but is increasingly acquiring *the nature of an investment which would result in increasing the national income* [author's emphasis]."[33] In the same year, OECD established its Educational Investment and Planning Programme which spurred central educational planning in member nations. The planning influenced member nations to think seriously about the relationship between their schools and economic growth and productivity.[34]

European Human Capital: Public Policy, Equal Education, and Protecting Cultural Traditions

OECD's European economists, unlike some University of Chicago economists, did not consider turning schooling over to free market forces but retained a belief that it should be part of public policy. Also, unlike some American economists, they continued to believe in the importance of general education in contrast to simple education in employment skills. These OECD economists worried about the elite nature of their secondary and university systems in contrast to the supposed equality of educational opportunity offered in the US and the Soviet Union.

Writing the "Preface" for *Policy Conference on Economic Growth and Investment in Education Washington 16th–20th October 1961*, OECD Secretary-General from 1960–1969 Thorkil Kristensen, a Danish economist, asserted that its members believed, "economic expansion has become the watchword of governments and peoples all over the world."[35] The Secretary-General argued that a main problem in achieving this goal was the "scarcity of qualified manpower."[36] National economies, he believed, were dependent on the application of scientific knowledge to production to spur economic growth. Building a cadre of educated people was key to this process. Kristensen captured the heart of future efforts of OECD: "Any educational effort, if it is to be fruitful, obviously involves planning; and the great difficulty in planning an educational policy is that it must look so far ahead."[37]

The commitment of OECD to human capital economics was highlighted in the book by Swedish economist Ingvar Svennilson in conjunction with German educational researcher Friedrich Edding and British educationist Lionel Elvin. Their introduction stated an often heard refrain of OECD documents, "Education is also more and more widely recognized as a means to economic growth which, since the end of the war, has everywhere become a paramount aim of national policy."[38]

The book confronted the problem of how to maintain a commitment to freedom of choice while at the same time linking education to national manpower needs. These economists emphasized the importance of education remaining part of government public policy. However, there appeared to be a conflict between individual choice and the desire of governments to accomplish manpower goals. In offering a resolution to this problem, Svennilson and his colleagues placed their faith in the "market" to persuade students to study for a career needed by society. They also counted on vocational guidance to use predictions of future labor market to influence students. In their words, "Man is a social being, and a student is likely to be attracted to that kind of study and career in which he feels he will be most useful to society and most wanted by it. This tendency is strengthened by the market system."[39]

Svennilson and his colleagues identified as a major hindrance to manpower planning the elite bias and lack of equality of educational opportunity in European educational systems. They were concerned about elitist traditions regarding enrollments in secondary and higher education. Education for economic growth required expanding enrollments to these institutions. Some worried that expanding enrollments would lower the quality of secondary and higher education. The writers also expressed concern that the emphasis on science and technology would result in "the great heritage of European literary tradition . . . to some extent be[ing] neglected."[40]

They did not provide an answer for the dilemma of expanding enrollments without decreasing quality and suggested that future research might provide an answer. Citing research from Svennilson's Sweden, they suggested that there might be little effect on overall quality when "less able" students attend secondary schools and that there were positive aspects in "the social gain in educating those students together."[41] Citing the role of the American comprehensive high school in creating a sense of social unity, they pointed out that detractors of the American high school highlighted negative aspects on "abler students" of a comprehensive enrollment that included the "less able."

These OECD authors also reported concerns about the loss of general education with calls for specialized workers. Wanting to maintain a tradition of general education, the authors argued, "By and large it is the technologist who has spent longest on his general education who goes the furthest, mainly because he has a wider basis of knowledge and can apply it to a wider range of problems than can a specialist."[42]

However, despite concerns about quality, maintaining literary traditions, and the future of general education, Svennilson and his colleagues accepted the idea promulgated by the Chicago School of Economics that education is an investment with rates-of-return for both a nation and an individual. Therefore, national education plans need to select investments that yield the highest rate-of-return to the public by stimulating economic growth. Unlike some American economists, they argued against turning education planning over to market forces and privatization. However, if schools were run by private enterprise without subsidies, the adjustment of the system to technical, social and economic changes would in the nature of the case not necessarily coincide with national interest.

We have therefore to accept the fact that the development of education must be guided by public education policy.

Reflecting the emphasis of *Targets for Education in Europe in 1970s* on national education planning among European nations, OECD launched the Mediterranean Regional Project. The goal was linking the ministries of economics with the ministries of education in Greece, Italy, Portugal, Spain, Turkey, and Yugoslavia as part of expanding their education systems. Aid came from US specialists in human resource development, resulting in a so-called "manpower approach" to educational planning.[43]

OECD: Statistics, Global Standardization, and Measurement

In 1964 at the fourth Conference on Economic Growth and Investment in Education a resolution was passed creating a model handbook for "the various factors involved in effective educational planning, so that countries represented may have the basis for the compilation of comparable statistics."[44] The handbook was a precursor to later annual compilation of educational statistics that helped to globalize educational policies. In addition, the handbook introduced mathematical models for linking education with economic planning and labor and production needs. It also began the practice of making international comparisons which would eventually reach their high point with the publication, in the 1990s, of comparative results from their international testing program.

The problem of comparing educational systems was simplified when OECD adopted UNESCO's 1976 International Standard Classification of Education (ISCED). UNESCO claimed, "ISCED provides a systematic structure for assembling international statistics of education . . . to improve international comparability of the statistics."[45] This classification system contributed both to the spread of human capital education ideas and to the global standardization of education. The original UNESCO 1976 document explained its purpose: "It is expected to facilitate international compilation and comparison of education statistics as such and also *their use in conjunction with manpower and other economic statistics . . . [and] should facilitate the use of education statistics in manpower planning and encourage the use of manpower statistics in educational planning* [author's emphasis]."[46] Also, UNESCO's classifications were meant to work with the International Standard Classification of Occupations (ISCO) which was created by a 1957 meeting of the International Conference of Labour Statisticians.[47]

The creators of ISCED were surprised at the already existing uniformity of global education and subjects. In a previous book, I detail the causes and evolution of global similarities of national schools systems.[48] The UNESCO report stated, "Thus despite variability in duration of so-called 'primary' and 'secondary' school programmes in different countries, the total number of years spent from school entry to university graduation is remarkably consistent from country to country, being 16 or 17 years in almost all cases."[49] Based on existing similarities between countries, UNESCO created a classification scheme that included an educational ladder leading from primary education through university education. They found a remarkable similarity in subjects taught at the primary level. ISCED provided OECD with the basis for classifying national education statistics and making comparisons of costs, enrollments, teachers, and other characteristics. Eventually, this would include comparisons of scores on OECD tests. In summary, OECD by the 1970s was busy pushing a human capital agenda for education and contributing to the globalization of educational standards.

Education Inflation and the Oversupply of College Graduates

A problem, which would continue to haunt education planners, was that the drive to expand education systems to stimulate economic growth and productivity resulted in more school graduates than could be absorbed by the national labor markets. The question never seemed to be raised by the originators of human capital theories that there might be limits on the number of school graduates that could find employment at the level of their credentials. The result was education inflation or the declining economic value of education credentials. Also, the student revolts in the 1960s called into question the idea of sending so many to college. The result was reflected in the 1976 publication of Richard Freeman's *The Overeducated American*.[50] Freeman argued that the flood of college graduates in the 1960s and 1970s was reducing, contrary to expectations of early human capital economists, the rate-of-return on investment in education. Concerns about rates-of-return would continue into the twenty-first century. A 1978 review of Freeman's book distributed by the Rand Corporation, a private research firm with US government contracts, highlights the ongoing debate about human capital.

> The Overeducated American. Freeman argues that income returns from college have declined so rapidly since 1970 that from both a private and social perspective additional investments in college training will be marginal at best and are likely to remain so for many years to come. On the basis of our reexamination of the wage and employment data since the 1970s, we will argue that at best Freeman exaggerates the case of an oversupply of college-educated manpower and that he may in fact be wrong. The data for the 1970s are clearly telling a fascinating story of adjustments to large entering cohorts. But to us it is a story of an overcrowded new entrant and not an overeducated American. The absence of any reduction in the relative wages of more experienced college workers during this decade represents a serious challenge to Freeman's hypothesis.[51]

OECD: Human Capital and the Economization of Everyday Life

Student unrest in the 1960s and 1970s, unemployment of college graduates, the international migration of workers, and the first world oil crisis in the 1970s resulted in OECD publications combining human capital goals with those for maintaining social order, or in the words of OECD documents, social cohesion. As I previously mentioned, social unity was a concern of the authors of *Targets for Education in Europe in 1970.*

The result was similar to the discussion in Chapter 1 of Gary Becker's application of economics to everyday life. Consequently, OECD did not abandon its original human capital goals, but began to work on socio-economic goals. OECD shifted its emphasis on education and economic growth to education as part of social service, which eventually included early childhood education, services to families, assimilation of foreign workers, support for women's rights, environmental education, and lifelong learning. Its educational policy statement for the 1970s reflected these social service issues, "Goals for educational growth in the 1970s should be made more explicit, and where possible indicators should be used which would measure the performance of the educational system, both in relation to educational goals as such *and the contribution to the wider social and economic objectives* [author's emphasis]."[52]

These broader socio-economic goals resulted in application of economic frameworks to preschool, families, the updating of employment skills (lifelong learning), and assimilation of foreign workers. It also included the difficult goal of achieving equality of educational opportunity using anti-poverty programs and preparing poor children for school learning with compensatory education programs, preschool, and social policies to help low-income families. The 1967 report "Social Objectives in Educational Planning" of The Study Group in the Economics of Education defined the following goals for non-compulsory secondary and higher education (most OECD nations had compulsory primary education):

1. Equal access to non-compulsory education for all youngsters of equivalent measured ability—regardless of sex, race, place of residence, social class, or other irrelevant criteria;
2. Equal rates of participation in non-compulsory education by members of all social classes;
3. Equal opportunity to acquire academic ability for youngsters of all social classes, i.e. effective participation of all social classes—the most stringent definition of all.[53]

Economization of teaching and lifelong learning became another OECD objective. Economization of teaching would eventually lead, in the twenty-first century, to calculating the effects of high- and low-quality teachers on a student's future income.[54] In addition, OECD studied teacher supply and demand and teacher training along with the economic planning of school systems and buildings. Lifelong education, which originated in Scandinavian countries having a long tradition of adult education, had the goal of "updating knowledge and counteracting obsolete qualifications" for employment.[55]

Human Capital: Social Service and Cohesion

In the twenty-first century, the social service aspects of human capital theory were highlighted in an OECD published book by Brian Keeley called, *Human Capital: How What You Know Shapes Your Life*.[56] In the book's opening pages, Keeley tells the story of Linda who lives in a Paris suburb with other North African immigrants. The suburb was the scene of youth riots that resulted in the burning of thousands of cars. Linda is described as being raised in a "traditionally minded North African family."[57] At a local community center, men are described as sitting around listening to rap music while Linda and three other unemployed women from differing ethnic backgrounds meet with an employment counselor. All the women complain that getting a job is difficult because of transportation problems and discrimination.

Linda regrets that her schooling was cut short even though she was a model student. Her father believed that women shouldn't work and that they should stay home until marriage. Consequently, her father withdrew her from school before she could graduate. Married as a teenager and later separated from her husband, she faces a potential life of unemployment. Faced with this situation, the author comments, "To get on, to get a better job and to improve their incomes, the women know they need to have an education."[58]

But in this story education is not just about getting a job. It is also about reducing the potential for more riots in French immigrant communities. Human capital is tied to both job skills and reducing community tensions by teaching shared values in schools. "Indeed," the author writes, "even the relationships and shared values in societies can be seen as a *form of capital* [social capital] that makes it easier for people to work together and achieve economic success."[59] As discussed in Chapter 1, social capital is the contribution of social interactions to economic growth and productivity.

Keeley refers to social capital as "networks together with shared norms, values and understandings that facilitate co-operation within and among groups."[60] Keeley describes three categories of social capital. The first category is the *bonds* that link people to a shared identity through family, close friends, and culture. The second are the *bridges* that link people to those who do not share a common identity. The last are the *linkages* that connect people to those up and down the social scale or, in other words, those from different social classes. It is important for Linda, Keeley argues, to help her create bridges to those outside the immigrant community as a means of increasing her social capital. Consequently, schools need to ensure an education that builds these bridges to others and linkages that reduce conflict between social classes.

Thus, Keeley's book reflects the broader notions of human capital and social service that appeared in OECD concerns after the 1970s. It isn't enough for Linda to receive an education to learn skills for employment. It also requires attention to social capital which in this case would allow Linda to use her education for employment. Developing human capital and social capital become part of OECD's economization of education which, as I describe in Chapter 6, become very important in proposals for preschool education and changing family life.

Expanding Human Capital

Keeley's *Human Capital* illustrates OECD's broadening of concerns about the interrelationship of factors affecting the global economy and the role of education. In this context, human capital includes all factors affecting the quality of the labor force. Originally, the focus was on the educational level of the workforce, but as the concept evolved among OECD researchers it included other elements impacting workers, such as health, migration, environmental degradation, urbanization, ageing, gender equality, and security. As part of human capital, the impact of these factors on workers and families was seen as affecting economic growth and productivity. In other words, similar to Gary Becker's work, human capital encompassed the economization of social life and the environment.

A good example of the expanded notion of human capital is OECD's publication *Trends Shaping Education 2013*, which relates education to issues such as global migration, the environment, urban living, security, health, working women, ageing societies, changing family structures, and technology.[61] The publication relates these global trends to possible educational responses.

Economic concerns were an important part of education's role in dealing with OECD's global trends. For instance, in response to the increasing global mobility of the world's peoples, the following questions are asked:

- Transferability of skills and experience is one of the big challenges for classrooms containing students from all over the world. Are our systems able to adequately recognize prior learning and qualifications? How should this be accomplished?
- Are educators equipped to deal with the inequality of educational opportunity that greater numbers of immigrants may cause?
- To what extent should high-income countries be concerned about skimming off the best and brightest from low-income countries?[62]

The above questions touch upon important economic and educational questions that go far beyond the original concerns of human capital economists of the 1950s and 1960s. The concern with the international transfer of education credentials could contribute to the trend of creating a world culture of schooling where national school systems are very similar. The question of inequality of educational opportunity is one that plagues many nations as illustrated in the previous discussion of Keeley's book. As I will discuss in Chapter 4 with regard to the World Bank, the movement of talent from poorer to richer nations has undermined the implementation of human capital plans in developing nations. The assumption that investment in schooling will stimulate economic growth is not supported when a developing nation expands its educational opportunities and then watches as their school graduates migrate to richer countries and jobs.

Trends Shaping Education 2013 also links education for national economic growth to the global economy in declaring: "Economies are increasingly intertwined and interdependent."[63] In this context, economization of education includes preparation of a global worker. For instance, the publication states, "Education and training systems have traditionally been bastions of national-decision making."[64] The fear is that national school systems will not prepare students to work in a global labor force. This is reflected in the question: "Do these [national] systems provide students with the necessary outlook and skills, including language skills, for successful international cooperation?"[65]

An element of realism is introduced when discussing economic setbacks. Early human capital economists promoted education as an economic panacea with the assumption that the primary issue was economic growth and productivity. In this OECD publication, education is called upon to help workers adjust to recessions and depressions: "How might education nurture the kind of transferable skills to cope and adapt to economic uncertainty and change?"[66] Similar economic questions are raised regarding an ageing population, lifelong learning, and economic inequalities: "Initial education and lifelong learning play a role in lifting people out of poverty by, for example, providing them with the right skills for the labor market. What kinds of programs . . . would strengthen this function of education?" "How aware are students in OECD countries of these larger global problems and should they know more about inequity and poverty world-wide?"[67]

OECD extends the economization of education to environmental concerns. OECD does this by referring to a "green economy" and raises the following educational questions:

- What kind of tertiary and post-secondary training might provide the skills and expertise needed for a green economy?
- Despite the progress shown here, there is an ongoing need to protect natural resources and biodiversity. What role does education have in shaping the knowledge, attitudes and behavior of young people on this issue?[68]

While economic issues are always in the background of social concerns, *Trends Shaping Education 2013* does speak to education's role in a range of other topics such as urbanization, traffic safety, and health. Obviously, schools can help recently arrived rural populations with their new urban environment by teaching traffic safety and how to live a healthy life. Gender equality is stated as an important global goal with attention being focused on gender stereotypes in the workplace. The question asked about the role of schools in promoting gender equity was: "What is the role of education in challenging negative assumptions and behaviors that are part of these stereotypes?"[69] As OECD broadened its meaning of human capital and educational concerns, it found a method for comparing the quality of human capital and educational systems.

From Manpower Planning to Test Scores

OECD researchers abandoned manpower planning methods as they broadened the concept of human capital. As mentioned previously, manpower planners in the 1960s and 1970s were faced with an oversupply of college graduates and the declining value of college degrees. This raised questions about the possibility of actually predicting future labor market needs and planning educational systems around these predictions. Eventually, the uncertainty of basing educational planning on manpower predictions was abandoned for a more generic approach relying on skills-based predications for the labor market and education based on test scores.

In the midst of student protests and unemployment of college graduates, OECD published a 1970s study questioning the idea of education planning based on manpower needs. The lengthy title indicated the scope of the study's work and OECD's worries about manpower planning: *Occupational and Educational Structures of the Labour Force and Levels of Economic Development: Possibilities and Limitations of an International Comparison Approach.*[70] The study warned of the "specter of oversupply of qualified personnel." As discussed previously, OECD's manpower planning utilized UNESCO's 1976 ISCED, and the International Conference of Labour Statisticians' 1957 ISCO, in trying to align manpower needs with educational systems.

The 1970 OECD study's preface expressed concern "with operationalizing the quantitative link between economic growth and educational expansion patterns."[71] It called it naive to use a quantified approach to manpower planning, such as predicting future needs for engineers, scientists, accountants, and other occupations and then engaging in education planning to fulfill those needs. In addition, educational planning was difficult because there also was a social demand to attend secondary school and college resulting from personal interests and/or family pressure.

Regarding educational planning, the study argued it would be difficult to use manpower planning and social demand to estimate the number of places needed for students, particularly in higher education. Citing another report, the study asserted in reference to planning based on occupational predictions: "we have found no reliable basis for reckoning the totality of such needs over a long term."[72] The pressure for linking future occupational demands to educational planning, according to the study:

> has led to a paradoxical situation: on the one hand we have seen a proliferation of long-term educational forecasts concentrating on a very few global and quantitative factors, such as total enrollments, number of graduates and school-leavers, total educational expenditure, etc. Demographic forecasts and, sometimes, manpower forecast constitute the guide posts with respect to the economy and the society in general . . . On the other hand, and at the same time, more qualitative changes are being introduced, such as the trend towards comprehensive education in many countries, curriculum reforms, technological changes. . . .[73]

In other words, educational planning based on manpower predictions deals with a future of unpredictable occupational changes and fluid school systems.

What to do with the unreliability of linking manpower planning with education planning? First, and this is what happened, drop the idea of a long-term prediction of manpower needs and replace it with a more generic term of "future skill-needs" of the workforce. In Chapter 3, I focus on the current global call to educate for particular skills. Second, determine the quality of educational systems and plan changes in those systems based on skills of graduates. In other words, create an international testing program to measure skills and influence local school systems to move to a curriculum based on the skills needed by employers.

Economization of Test Scores

PISA and TIMSS were developed to measure the cognitive skills learned in literacy and math programs and, consequently, the value of a nation's human capital. These skills are considered necessary for employment in a knowledge society. In addition, OECD developed the Programme for the International Assessment of Adult Competencies (PIAAC) designed to measure the human capital skills of a nation. I will discuss PIAAC in more detail in Chapter 3 which is devoted to the issue of skill-based education.

Consequently, PISA and TIMSS scores are used to measure the quality of a nation's labor force without using predictions of the number of possible college and high school graduates needed to meet future manpower requirements. A problem in devising the tests is the variations in curriculum and culture between nations. OECD claims that PISA tests general knowledge and skills needed by the economy without being tied to a particular school curriculum: "PISA is unique because it develops tests which are not directly linked to the school curriculum. The tests are designed to assess to what extent students at the end of compulsory education, can apply their knowledge to real-life situations and be equipped for full participation in society."[74]

TIMSS is designed to test knowledge about mathematics and science which, since the original manpower concerns of the 1950s and 1960s, is considered an important measure of the value of human capital. TIMSS measures mathematics and science achievement at the fourth and eighth grades. TIMSS is used, like PISA, "in various ways to explore educational issues, including: monitoring system-level achievement trends in a global context, establishing achievement goals and standards for educational improvement, stimulating curriculum reform, improving teaching and learning through research and analysis of the data, conducting related studies (e.g. monitoring equity or assessing students in additional grades), and training researchers and teachers in assessment and evaluation."[75]

In other words, scores on both PISA and TIMSS are supposed to influence the national education systems. Consequently, they contribute, as I will explain, to the growth of a world culture of schooling with increased similarities between national education systems. In this section, I will focus on PISA since the chapter is devoted to the work of OECD in spreading human capital ideas.

Since 2000, PISA has been given every three years to randomly selected 15-year-old students in schools throughout the world in what are considered the key subjects needed by the global economy, namely reading, math, and science. In 2012, "510,000 students in 65 economies took part in the PISA 2012 assessment of reading, mathematics and science representing about 28 million 15-year-olds globally. Of those economies, 44 took part in an assessment of creative problem solving and 18 in an assessment of financial literacy."[76] By 2014, students from 70 economies had participated in the test.[77]

Supposedly PISA assesses a student's ability to participate in today's society. OECD's official descriptive brochure explains, "PISA assesses the extent to which students near the end of compulsory education have acquired key knowledge and skills that are essential for full participation in modern societies."[78] PISA also gathers data on students' backgrounds and schools. The purpose of data collection is "to identify the factors that influence student performance."[79]

Given its global impact, the test is surprisingly short. OECD describes the assessment: "Paper-based tests were used, lasting two hours for each student. In some countries an extra 40 minutes were devoted to the computer-based assessment of mathematics, reading and problem solving. Questions were a mixture of multiple choice and those requiring students to construct their own responses."[80]

According to OECD, this 2 hour or 2 hours plus 40 minutes assessment covering reading, math, and science is supposed to help governments evaluate the work of their school system: "PISA helps stakeholders assess how well schools are equipping today's youth for adult life, whether education systems are fair, and whether some schools and teaching methods are more effective than others . . . Countries and economies participating in successive PISA cycles can compare the performance of their students over time and assess the impact of education policy decisions."[81]

What about students who don't care, tighten up during tests or are sick during the 2 hours of testing? I have not found an OECD response to this possibility. However, Hanushek, Woessman, and Peterson answer the question: "Defenders of standardized tests recognize their limitations for the evaluation of any one individual, but they claim that errors that occur at the individual level cancel one another out when results are aggregated for large groups."[82]

PISA scores are supposed to be a measure of the quality of a nation's human capital. In reporting the results of the 2012 administration of PISA, the Secretary-General of OECD, Angel Gurría, stressed the economic importance of the test scores: "Equipping young people with the skills to achieve their full potential, participate in an increasingly interconnected global economy, and ultimately convert better jobs into better lives is a central preoccupation of policy makers around the world."[83]

Politically, it would appear that authoritarian governments operate some of the top scoring school systems in the world. In 2012, the ten countries with the highest PISA scores were, in rank order, Shanghai-China, Singapore, Hong Kong-China, Chinese Taipei, Korea, Macao-China, Japan, Liechtenstein, Switzerland, and the Netherlands.[84]

Are China and Singapore to be models for world school systems based on their test scores? Paradoxically, considering the advocacy of free markets by American human capital economists, China practices "socialism with Chinese characteristics" and has free markets as part of a planned economy. In addition, China's education system is centrally controlled and closely censors school materials. The same is true of Singapore.[85]

Highlighting OECD's economic concerns was a 2012 assessment "Financial Literacy Skills for the 21st Century."[86] OECD claims financial literacy skills will help people adjust to economic problems: "Financial literacy is thus an essential life skill, and high on the global policy agenda. Shrinking welfare systems, shifting demographics, and the increased sophistication and expansion of financial services have all contributed to a greater awareness of the importance of ensuring that citizens and consumers of all ages are financially literate."[87]

"Financial literacy is an essential life skill for young people," declares OECD's report of the 2012 assessment.[88] Besides wanting to make economic growth and productivity a goal of schools, OECD wants more economic content taught in schools. This represents what I would call the economization of the school curriculum when financial literacy is combined with the World Economic Forum's advocacy of requiring entrepreneurship courses in colleges and secondary schools (as I discuss in Chapter 5). Of the 13 participating countries students in Shanghai-China received the highest scores on the financial literacy test. As a result of what were considered overall low scores, OECD urged that financial literacy be included in national curricula, further economizing the schools. Young people on the brink of adulthood are poised to make complex financial decisions that will have an impact on the rest of their lives.

Results from the PISA 2012 financial literacy assessment show that many students, including those living in countries that are high-performers in the main PISA assessment, need to improve their financial literacy.[89]

As a gauge of the quality of human capital, OECD explicitly wants the result of its tests to influence policymakers. The organization asserts, "Policy makers use PISA results to gauge the knowledge and skills of students in their own countries in comparison with those in other countries, set policy targets against measurable goals achieved by other education systems, and learn from policies and practices applied elsewhere."[90]

PISA and its Contribution to a World Culture of Schooling

A 2012 study confirmed the influence of PISA scores on local schools. The study found that 21 countries changed their school practices as the result of test scores on PISA and TIMSS.[91] As part of a general pattern of globalization, reactions to the scores speeded along the process of creating uniformity between national schools and contributed to a worldwide culture of schooling. National education planners wanting to improve test scores utilized international education proposals and changes adopted by other school systems. Sociologist David H. Kamens, in writing about PISA, describes this process: "the institutionalization of education leads to continuous and intensified efforts to improve it. High volumes of education reform are thus characteristics of the modern world system. In this environment a good deal of *standardization* occurs across countries."[92]

In a broader context, this means that the educational goals behind PISA and TIMSS to improve human capital and focus on the education of future workers contribute to a growing standardization of a global education system. This raises the issue of the cultural impact of changes in national school systems as a result of scores on PISA and TIMSS.

Are national school systems primarily educating students for a global corporate culture and is this resulting in growing standardization of world cultures? Culture, as sociologist Kamens points out, has an effect on test scores. He argues that China scores high because of an exam-oriented culture with schools emphasizing memorization and rote learning. The same could be said of Korea with its strong Confucian exam-oriented tradition. Kamens also points out the major cultural differences and educational practices between China and Switzerland with both countries having high scores. Kamens asserts that when education officials look for "best practices" to adopt to raise test scores there is an assumption: "that education is like engineering . . . One of the problems with the current search for 'best practices' is that it often overlooks important features of the contexts in which these practices are embedded."[93] Over the long run, could the adoption of "best practices" change local cultural contexts?

Questions about global education standardization and the cultural impact of PISA are raised by Heinz-Dieter Meyer and Aaron Benavot in their Introduction to *PISA, Power, and Policy: The Emergence of Global Educational Governance*. The two authors present the following issues that they consider as common themes in the essays about PISA in their book.

- How, and through which interested actors, is PISA being institutionalized as a global mode of education governance?
- What key legitimizing beliefs and assumptions are being established and to what extent are they contests?
- What are the organization and policy consequences of this new political regime for education being ushered in worldwide?[94]

Based on the possibility that PISA is contributing to a world culture of schooling based on the occupational needs of global corporations, I would ask the following questions:

- Is PISA contributing a world culture of schools primarily concerned with educating corporate workers?
- Is PISA contributing to a standardization of world cultures that reflect the internal cultures of multinational corporations?

OECD, PISA, and the Economization of Schools

The United States is one example of the effect of PISA scores. The following questions can be asked of the work of some American economists who claim that US students' low PISA scores predict a future economic disaster.

- Are PISA test scores predictors of future economic growth and productivity?
- Should a 2 hour or a 2 hour plus 40 minute test covering the broad subjects of reading, math, and science given to students in widely disparate school systems and cultures determine changes in national school policies?
- How are PISA test scores being used to increase the economization of education?

First, I want to emphasize that students taking PISA are not yet part of the economy. Whether their scores are high or low says nothing about existing economic conditions since these students are not usually participants in the workforce and after graduation will not immediately improve or hurt the quality of human capital.

Even the previously cited economists and political scientist, Hanushek, Peterson, and Woessman, who use PISA scores to illustrate the title of their book

Endangering Prosperity: A Global View of the American School, admit that it takes 40 years for students impacted by school reforms resulting from PISA scores to have an impact on the economy. First, they argue, there is the time required to implement a school reform. Second, they write, "the economic impact of improved skills will not be realized until the students with greater skills move into the labor force . . . Thus even after an education reform is fully implemented, it takes some forty years until the full labor force is at the new skill level."[95]

Forty years! As suggested in criticisms of human capital theory in Chapter 1 a lot happens in a 40-year period that effects economic conditions, such as depressions and recessions, natural disasters, war, environmental conditions, revolutions, and changes in consumer tastes and life style. Despite the uncertainty in making any long-term economic predictions, Hanushek, Peterson, and Woessman make them for an 80-year period from 2013 to 2093 based on changes in school policies designed to raise PISA test scores. Their economic projections are based on a child being born in 2013 and attending schools that have changed to ensure higher test scores.

In making these predictions, the authors equate test scores with "cognitive skills." They assume that without educational changes—like other human capital economists they assume that schooling is a key factor in economic growth—the US economy will grow at 1.5 percent a year over an 80-year period. What happens, they ask, to US economic growth if test scores are raised to the level of Germany, Canada, and Singapore?

Before reporting their conclusions, I would like to remind the reader that it is questionable whether or not a 2 hour test can predict the future conditions of an economy and whether or not economists can make accurate 80-year predictions. They conclude, "Reaching Germany's performance level would lift the GDP per capita in 2093 to 25 percent above that it would obtain if no gains in student performance were realized . . . In terms of individual workers, it amounts to an increase in every worker's income of 12 percent every year for the next eighty years."[96]

Eric Hanushek, one of the authors of *Endangering Prosperity,* is a well-known education economist working at Stanford University and the Hoover Institute. On his university website, his narrative biography states, "His pioneering analysis measuring teacher quality through the growth in student achievement forms the basis for current research into the value-added of teachers and schools . . . Most recently, Hanushek shows that the quality of education is closely related to national economic growth."[97]

His human capital approach and emphasis on teacher quality is reflected in the conclusion of *Endangering Prosperity* and in other works. For instance, Hanushek opens an article titled "Valuing Teachers: How much is a teacher worth?" with the often stated refrain in the US: "For some time, we have recognized that the academic achievement of schoolchildren in this country threatens . . . ultimately its success in the global economy. The low achievement of American students, as reflected in . . . PISA, will prevent them from accessing good, high-paying jobs."[98]

Applying economic models linking teacher quality (as measured by their students' test scores) and PISA scores with lifetime earnings, Hanushek concludes: "A good, but not great, teacher increases each student's lifetime earnings by $10,600. Given a class of 20 students, she will raise their aggregate earnings by $212,000."[99] This statement highlights the economization of test scores and the attempts to link them with economic growth and personal income. Like the economy it is difficult to know what life and the economy will be like in the future.

Hanushek presses his argument by asking what the effect of increasing the quality of teachers would be on overall economic growth. It is important to remember that teacher quality in this case is measured by her/his students' test scores. In making this calculation, Hanushek emphasizes the assumptions of human capital economics: "student achievement [as measured by PISA scores], which *provides a direct measure of later quality of the labor force*, is strongly related to economic growth. Improving achievement [test scores] leads to a better prepared workforce and to greater growth [author's emphasis]."[100]

So how much is a teacher worth to economic growth when they raise their students' PISA scores? Hanushek estimates that if teacher quality were improved so that student PISA scores were close to those of Finland it would increase "the annual growth rate of the United States by 1 percent GDP. Accumulated over the lifetime of somebody born today, this improvement in achievement would amount to nothing less than an increase in total U.S. economic output of $112 trillion in present value."[101]

The important point for this book is the economization of OECD's PISA test scores to predict economic growth and personal income, and to evaluate teacher quality. In addition, PISA test scores are politicized with Hanushek, Peterson, and Woessman listing an agenda in *Endangering Prosperity* that includes reducing the power of teachers' unions and changing state laws regarding tenure and teacher evaluations. They criticize calls for changing tax laws to reduce the income inequalities, and offer improving teacher quality (improved student PISA scores) as the panacea for reducing inequalities. In the concluding paragraph of their book, they present the human capital argument (with skill meaning scores on PISA) which avoids income redistribution in favor of improving student test scores.

> The upward shift in the growth rate of the American economy that would accompany a more highly skilled population can resolve most if not all of the fiscal and distributional problems on the table today. Even more, it would enhance the lives, enjoyment of liberties, and the opportunity for happiness on the part of its citizens.[102]

Conclusion

By the twenty-first century PISA and TIMSS scores were considered indicators of the quality of national education systems and human capital. A 2 hour or 2 hour plus 40 minute PISA test covering reading, math, and science given in a variety of cultures has come to dominate discussions of the effect of schools on national economies. For example, as discussed in Chapter 1, the United States reacted to arguments that schools were undermining the economy by instituting Common Core State Standards to raise test scores and to make workers more competitive in the global economy.

As the "World Ministry" of education, OECD disseminated human capital ideas and, like Gary Becker, broadened the meaning to include most aspects of everyday life. It also abandoned ideas of manpower planning and focused on measuring the general quality of a nation's workforce by test scores. These actions contributed to a standardization of global education and creation of a world culture of schooling. Also, OECD test scores were used by economists to make questionable predictions about a nation's economic future.

Both early members of the Chicago School and OECD officials expressed concern about education credentials being good predictors of a person's economic worth. Numbers of years of schooling could not predict, it was argued, the future value of human capital. Reliance on simply getting more people into schools to attain higher credentials had resulted in education inflation and an oversupply of college graduates. Consequently, there was a shift in argument from years of schooling to the actual skills learned. This resulted in a reliance on measuring skill levels by test scores with the assumption that PISA scores reflected the skill level of a nation and were good predictors of economic health.

In the next chapter, I will discuss skills as the "new global currency." The focus on skills and tests changes the traditional reliance on brick and mortar schools. All forms of schooling can be justified as long as they produce high test results and teach workplace skills. But how do you determine what skills are needed in the future labor market? Are skills determined by what global businesses want? Does the focus on skills and test scores result in a worker unprepared to protect themselves from potential exploitation by global corporations?

Notes

1 Eric A. Hanushek, Paul E. Peterson, and Ludger Woessman, *Endangering Prosperity: A Global View of the American School* (Washington, DC: Brookings Institution Press, 2013), p. 29.
2 David H. Kamens, "Globalization and the Emergence of an Audit Culture: PISA and the search for 'best practices' and magic bullets" in *Pisa, Power, and Policy: The Emergence of Global Educational Governments* edited by Heinz-Dieter Meyer and Aaron Benavot (Oxford: Symposium Books, 2013), p. 123.
3 George S. Papadopoulos, *Education 1960–1990: The OECD Perspective* (Paris: OECD, 1994), p. 21.
4 OECD, "Our Mission." Retrieved from http://www.oecd.org/about/ on October 14, 2013.
5 Ibid.
6 OECD, "Members and Partners." Retrieved from http://www.oecd.org/about/ membersandpartners/ on February 15, 2014.

7 OECD, "Mission." Retrieved from http://www.oecd.org/about/ on February 15, 2014.

8 OECD, "Members and Partners . . . ."

9 International Association for the Evaluation of Educational Achievement, "Brief History of IEA." Retrieved from http://www.iea.nl/brief_history_iea.html on January 28, 2008.

10 PISA, "Background and Basics." Retrieved from http://www.oecd.org/pisa/pisafaq/#background_and_basics on October 17, 2013.

11 Ibid.

12 Hanushek et al., *Endangering Prosperity* . . . , p. 31.

13 Papadopoulos, *Education 1960–1990* . . . , pp. 21–37.

14 Joel Spring, *The Sorting Machine Revisited: National Educational Policy Since 1945* Updated Edition (New York: Longman, 1989), pp. 35–93.

15 Daniel Barbezat, "The Marshall Plan and the Origin of the OEEC" in *OECD Historical Series: Explorations in OEEC History* edited by Richard T. Griffiths (Paris: OECD, 1997), pp. 15–33.

16 David W. Ellwood, "The Marshall Plan and the Politics of Growth" in *OECD Historical Series: Explorations in OEEC History* edited by Richard T. Griffiths (Paris: OECD, 1997), p. 101.

17 Ibid., p. 102.

18 Ibid., p. 102.

19 Bent Boel, "The European Productivity Agency, 1953–1961" in *OECD Historical Series: Explorations in OEEC History* edited by Richard T. Griffiths (Paris: OECD, 1997), pp. 113–122.

20 See Spring, *The Sorting Machine Revisited* . . . , pp. 35–63.

21 Ibid., pp. 63–92.

22 Papadopoulos, *Education 1960–1990* . . . , p. 26.

23 Ibid., p. 27.

24 Papadopoulos, *Education 1960–1990* . . . , p. 38.

25 Ibid., p. 41.

26 Richard T. Griffiths, "'An Act of Creative Leadership': The End of the OEEC and the Birth of OECD" in *OECD Historical Series: Explorations in OEEC History* edited by Richard T. Griffiths (Paris: OECD, 1997), pp. 235–257.

27 Angel Gurría, "Editorial," *Education at a Glance* (Paris: OECD, 2011), p. 16.

28 OECD, "About." Retrieved from http://www.oecd.org/about/ on August 7, 2014.

29 OECD, Convention on the Organization for Economic Co-operation and Development (December 14, 1960). Retrieved from http://www.oecd.org/general/conventionontheorganisationforeconomicco-operationanddevelopment.htm on August 7, 2014.

30 Ibid.

31 Papadopoulos, *Education 1960–1990* . . . , p. 38.

32 Ibid., p. 38.

33 Ibid., p. 40.

34 Ibid., pp. 47–49.

35 Thorkil Kristensen, "Preface" in Ingvar Svennilson, Friedrich Edding, and Lionel Elvin *Policy Conference on Economic Growth and Investment in Education Washington 16th–20th October 1961: Targets for Education in Europe in 1970* (Paris: OECD, 1962), p. 5.

36 Ibid., p. 5.

37 Ibid., p. 7.

38 Ibid., p. 15.

39 Ibid., p. 20.

40 Ibid., pp. 31–32.

41 Ibid., p. 32.

42 Ibid., p. 34.

43 Papadopoulos, *Education 1960–1990* . . . , pp. 43–46.

44 Ibid., p. 50.

45 UNESCO, "International Standard Classification of Education" (Paris: UNESCO Division of Statistics on Education, Office of Statistics, 1976), p. 15. Retrieved from http://unesdoc.unesco.org/images/0002/000209/020992eb.pdf on August 9, 2014.

46 Ibid., p. 1.

47 International Labour Organization, "International Standard Classification of Occupations." Retrieved from http://www.ilo.org/public/english/bureau/stat/isco/ on August 9, 2014.

48 See Joel Spring, *Pedagogies of Globalization: The Rise of the Educational Security State* (Mahwah, NJ: Lawrence Erlbaum, 2006).

49 UNESCO, "International Standard Classification of Education . . . ," pp. 5–6.

50 Richard Freeman, *The Overeducated American* (New York: Academic Press, 1976).

51 James P. Smith and Finis Welch, "The Overeducated American? A review article," The Rand Corporation 1978. Retrieved from http://www.rand.org/pubs/papers/P6253.html on August 9, 2014.

52 As quoted in Papadopoulos, *Education 1960–1990* . . . , p. 70.

53 As quoted in Ibid., p. 107.

54 See Eric A. Hanushek, "Valuing Teachers: How Much is a Good Teacher Worth?" *Education Next* (Summer 2011), pp. 40–45. Retrieved from http://hanushek.stanford.edu/publications/valuing-teachers-how-much-good-teacher-worth on August 13, 2014.

55 Papadopoulos, *Education 1960–1990* . . . , p. 112.

56 Brian Keeley, *Human Capital: How What You Know Shapes Your Life* (Paris: OECD Publishing, 2007), p. 14.

57 Ibid., p. 10.

58 Ibid., p. 11.

59 Ibid., p. 11.

60 Ibid., p. 103.

61 OECD, *Trends Shaping Education 2013* (Paris: OECD Publishing, 2013).

62 Ibid., p. 21.

63 Ibid., p. 25.

64 Ibid., p. 25.

65 Ibid., p. 25.

66 Ibid., p. 25.

67 Ibid., p. 33.

68 Ibid., p. 31.

69 Ibid., p. 57.

70 OECD, *Occupational and Educational Structures of the Labour Force and Levels of Economic Development: Possibilities and Limitations of an International Comparison Approach* (Paris: OECD Publishing, 1970).

71 Ibid., p. 5.

72 Ibid., p. 254.

73 Ibid., p. 256

74 OECD, "About PISA." Retrieved from http://www.oecd.org/pisa/aboutpisa/ on August 20, 2014.

75 TIMSS & PIRLS International Study Center, "About TIMSS and PIRLS." Retrieved from http://timssandpirls.bc.edu/ on August 20, 2014.

76 OECD, "About PISA . . . ."

77 Ibid.

78 OECD, "Programme for International Student Assessment (PISA)." Brochure retrieved from http://www.oecd.org/pisa/aboutpisa/PISA-trifold-brochure-2014.pdf on August 20, 2014.

79 Ibid.

80 Ibid.

81 Ibid.

82 Hanushek et al., *Endangering Prosperity* . . . , p. 88.

83 OECD, *PISA 2012 Results in Focus What 15-year-olds know and what they can do with what they know* (2014), p. 2. Retrieved from http://www.oecd.org/pisa/keyfindings/pisa-2012-results-overview.pdf on August 20, 2014.

84 Ibid., p. 5.

85 See Joel Spring, *Education and the Rise of the Global Economy* (Mahwah, NJ: Lawrence Erlbaum Associates, 1998), pp. 71–83 and Spring, *Pedagogies of Globalization* . . . , pp. 28–50, 190–237.

86 OECD, *PISA 2012 Results: Students and Money* (Paris: OECD Publishing, 2014). Retrieved from http://dx.doi.org/10.1787/9789264208094-en on August 20, 2014.

87 Ibid., p. 13.

88 Ibid., p. 118.

89 Ibid., p. 117.

90 OECD, "Programme for International Student Assessment . . . ."

91 David H. Kamens, "Globalization and the Emergence of an Audit Culture . . . ," p. 133.

92 Ibid., p. 134.

93 Ibid., p. 130.

94 Heinz-Dieter Meyer and Aaron Benavot, "Introduction: PISA and the Globalization of Education Governance: Some Puzzles and Problems" in *Pisa, Power, and Policy: The Emergence of Global Educational Government* . . . , p. 11.

95 Hanushek et al., *Endangering Prosperity* . . . , p. 59.

96 Ibid., pp. 62–63.

97 Eric A. Hanushek, Paul and Jean Hanna Senior Fellow Hoover Institute Stanford University, "Narrative Biography." Retrieved from http://hanushek.stanford.edu/eah/narrative-biography on August 21, 2014.

98 Eric Hanushek, "Valuing Teachers: How much is a teacher worth?," Education Next (Summer 2011), p. 41.

99 Ibid., p. 42.

100 Ibid., p. 43.

101 Ibid., p. 43.

102 Hanushek et al., *Endangering Prosperity* . . . , p. 103.

3

SKILLS

The New Global Currency

"Skills have become the global currency of twenty-first century economies," declared OECD's publication *Trends Shaping Education 2013*.[1] Economization of education has made teaching "skills" a twenty-first-century priority. In Chapter 1, I discussed concerns with skill instruction that emerged from human capital economic theory and the desire to identify the skills learned in schools that contribute to economic growth. Consequently, later economists focused on skills-based schooling in contrast to emphasizing the knowledge learned in traditional subjects. I will remind the reader that hard skills usually refer to such things as literacy instruction and numeracy along with specific job skills, and soft skills refer to character traits that will help the worker succeed in the workplace. Teaching soft skills was illustrated in Chapter 1 by Patrick Flanery's novel *Fallen Land* where the charter school, the Pinwheel Academy, inculcated soft skills or character traits required for corporate discipline.

There are cultural variations in the meaning of soft skills. For instance, the meaning of teamwork, frequently mentioned as an important corporate soft skill, varies between nations. Seán Ó Riain, a sociologist at the National University of Ireland, compares the meaning of teamwork in Japan, Sweden, and the US. In Japan, teamwork is considered as a means "for management to mobilize the knowledge and effort of workers."[2] While in Sweden teamwork is considered as a means of maintaining worker solidarity "to safeguard worker autonomy from management."[3] In the US, teamwork is "seen as a way to build up the record and skills that could be the basis of individual career advancement" without, as in Japan, a corporate commitment to "employment security."[4] Also, in contrast to the US, in Sweden teamwork promotes worker solidarity that can contribute to union protections and employment security.

Today, the OECD, the World Bank, and the World Economic Forum are globally promoting skills-based schooling with many nations aligning their curricula to skills considered necessary for employment and economic growth. OECD defines skills as the "ability to do something" which could include the ability to operate a machine (hard skill) or the ability to get along with others (soft skill).[5] Skills-based instruction, it is claimed, will solve most economic problems, including economic development and growth, unemployment, and inequalities in wealth. In Chapter 6, I will discuss the attempt to shape family life to develop in children the soft skills needed for work and for learning hard skills in school.

There are many questions surrounding the concept of skills. Are these skills to be general skills required by the economy or skills specifically related to a particular job or trade? What role do cultural differences make in teaching skills or are skills to be global and unrelated to a specific culture? Will skill instruction solve other global problems, such as protection of human rights and the environment? And, most importantly, is there a global skills gap?

The World Economic Forum's report "Education and Skills 2.0" highlights the confusion over the question of a skills gap:

> One arena in which accountability matters hugely is the effort to ensure that the skills imparted by an education system match those needed by employers. This issue has recently come to prominence because of the large number of reports from American National Association of Colleges and Employers who say they cannot find workers who have the skills needed to perform specific jobs even when pay levels are high. *Many economists, by contrast, say that the empirical evidence does not support the existence of any significant skills gap.* This is an issue that is unresolved in countries at all income levels [author's emphasis].[6]

In this chapter, I will discuss the surveys of the hard and soft skills wanted by global businesses and efforts to make skills education an important part of national school curricula.

The Skills Wanted by Global Businesses

High on the list of what corporations say they want is a person who is able to work in a team. "The Job Outlook for The Class of 2014," issued by the American National Association of Colleges and Employers, lists the most important skill wanted by businesses as "Ability to work in a team structure" followed in rank order by "Ability to make decisions and solve problems" and "Ability to plan organize, and prioritize work."[7] Fourth on the list is "Ability to verbally communicate with persons inside and outside the organization."[8] The other six skills identified desired by employers are:

1. Ability to obtain and process information
2. Ability to analyze quantitative data
3. Technical knowledge related to the job
4. Proficiency with computer software programs
5. Ability to create and/or edit written reports
6. Ability to sell or influence others.[9]

In summary, the American National Association of Colleges and Employers illustrates the importance placed on corporate teamwork. The hard skills desired by employers in this survey could be taught in any subject in school curricula including skills like decision making, prioritizing work tasks, and processing information. The organization lists hard skills specifically related to literacy, such as communication and ability to create and write corporate reports, and to math, such as ability to analyze data. Specific job-related hard skills are technical knowledge and proficiency with computer software.

Adecco, an employment management firm with 6,600 global offices, reports that employers list soft skills as being more important than hard skills.[10] In their 2013 report "The Skills Gap and the State of the Economy," surveyed senior executives (44%) claimed that soft skills were the major skills gap in finding workers as compared to technical skills (22%), leadership skills (14%), and computer skills (12%). For soft skills, Adecco listed "communication, critical thinking, creativity and collaboration."[11] It should be noted that Adecco's list is somewhat different from others with "communication" being listed as a soft skill while it is considered a hard skill, as I explain later in this chapter, by OECD (listening, speaking, reading, and writing)[12] and in most other contexts it is included as a literacy. Critical thinking and creativity are thought processes which, in this case, are treated as soft skills while others might list them as hard skills. Adecco's "collaboration" soft skill is the same as other calls for teamwork skills.

Another global employment manager, the ManpowerGroup, with offices in 80 countries and territories provides a different list of skills wanted by employers. Its skills survey includes 40,000 employers in 42 countries and represents one of the most extensive attempts to identify skills wanted by employers.[13] The ManpowerGroup, reporting on the reasons global companies are having trouble filling jobs, listed at the top: "Lack of technical competencies (hard skills)," (reported by 34 percent of companies), and "Lack of available applicants" (reported by 32 percent of companies).[14] The lack of available applicants might be caused by job candidates not having the right technical skills and/or a labor shortage. "Lack of workplace competencies (soft skills)" was reported by 19 percent of global companies.[15] The employers in this survey identified soft skills as "enthusiasm/motivation (5 percent), interpersonal skills (4 percent), professionalism (e.g. appearance, punctuality) (4 percent), and flexibility and adaptability (4 percent)."[16]

None of the above surveys indicate any desire for the knowledge learned in colleges from a traditional liberal arts curriculum or in traditional subjects in primary and secondary education except for job-related technical knowledge, literacy, and math skills. The teaching of general knowledge about governments, cultures, economies, and social structures becomes simply a vehicle for learning thinking skills needed by corporations. In this context, knowledge becomes secondary to skills training. The ManpowerGroup's list of soft skills is comparable to those of other surveys in this section.

It is important to note that there is no mention by employers in this survey of specific school content areas, such as history, literature, political science, economics, or the arts. The specific areas of knowledge mentioned are related to computers and job-related technical knowledge. These surveys suggest that learning skills is more important than content knowledge, which might result in the teaching of specific subjects such as history, literature, political science, economics, and the arts, as being the development of skills related to prioritizing tasks and processing information. Also, literacy skills focus not on a particular body of knowledge but on communication skills and writing corporate reports. What a student knows about the content of traditional subjects, other than math, is treated as irrelevant to the skills learned.

The emphasis on job-related skills might be causing a decline of enrollments in liberal arts curricula and in liberal arts colleges. The ManpowerGroup report lists the following top ten jobs global employers are having difficulty filling:

1. Skilled trade workers
2. Engineers
3. Sales representatives
4. Technicians
5. Accounting
6. Management/executives
7. IT staff
8. Drivers
9. Secretaries, PAs, administrative assistants & office support staff
10. Laborers

One might speculate that only sales representatives, management executives and secretaries, administrative assistants and office support staff could possibly benefit from a liberal arts education in seeking employment and in their corporate social interactions. On the other hand, many jobs in the list require specific training in a trade or a profession like engineering, accounting, and information. Two of the top ten, drivers and laborers, require only minimum hard skills.

Bemoaning the decline in liberal arts education, Victor E. Ferrall Jr., President Emeritus of Beloit College and author of Liberal Arts at the Brink, is quoted by Inside Higher Ed: "The problem is not that some places that call themselves 'liberal arts colleges' really aren't any more, but rather that the number of Americans who see the great value a liberal arts education provides is dwindling . . . In today's market, how is anyone going to get a job as an anthropologist or historian, let alone as a philosopher or expert in 19th-century English literature?"[17] Ferrall suggests that some traditional liberal arts programs are attempting to survive by claiming they teach thinking skills valuable to employers.

At my institution, the City University of New York (CUNY), the teaching of employment skills was emphasized in the implementation of new undergraduate general education requirements called "Pathways." The "Frequently Asked Questions" section of CUNY's Website includes: "How does the Pathways general education framework support the development of communication skills in students, the skills that employers state are the most desirable for potential employees?" The university's official answer is:

> The CUNY-wide Pathways general education framework learning outcomes specify that every Common Core course must build students' skills in producing well-reasoned written or oral arguments using evidence to support conclusions. Prior to Pathways, most CUNY colleges emphasized writing skills only in the portion of the general education curriculum that was composed of English Composition courses. Now, these skills are embedded within Pathways courses in widely varying fields, such as in a course in Africana, Puerto Rican and Latino Studies titled "Language and Ethnic Identity," and in a Biology course titled "The Science of Nutrition," both of which involve work on student communication skills.[18]

Except for English composition, math, and science, CUNY's Pathways shows little concern about the actual content of disciplines by proposing generic topics with faculty organizing the content around specific required skills. The required general education requirements of the largest urban university in the United States are:

> Required Common Core (12 credits/4 courses)
>   English Composition (2 courses)
>   Mathematical and Quantitative Reasoning (1 course)
>   Life and Physical Sciences (1 course)
>
> Flexible Common Core (18 credits/6 courses)
>   World Cultures and Global Issues (1 course)
>   U.S. Experience in Its Diversity (1 course)
>   Creative Expression (1 course)
>   Individual and Society (1 course)
>   Scientific World (1 course)[19]

In summary, educational institutions are adapting to demands by global businesses for workers with the right skills. Except for basic math and literacy skills and those related to specific occupations, such as information technology, most of the hard skills wanted by global corporations involve mental processes, such as prioritizing work tasks, processing information, decision making, leadership skills, and solving problems. Not surprisingly, businesses want the soft skills needed to ensure a profitable corporate life, such as teamwork and cooperation, punctuality, and enthusiasm/motivation. These soft skills, I will argue, are related to the attempt to develop a global corporate personality that might be in conflict with local cultures. In Chapter 6, I discuss cultural differences related to corporate soft skills.

In the next section, I discuss the skills gap in the context of economic conditions. As I suggested in Chapter 1, broader economic, social and political conditions are often neglected as economists and others call for economic remedies such as reducing the skills gap between what businesses wants and the education of human capital.

Is a Skills Gap Causing Unemployment and Labor Shortages?

The so-called skills gap varies between countries depending on economic conditions. In some countries there is simply a lack of jobs, while in other situations there is a lack of skilled workers. However, most employment needs appear to depend on conditions within a particular national economy. The following examples of Japan, Brazil, South Africa, Spain, and Ireland are related to the general global economy, particularly the effects of the 2008 global recession. I will not discuss these broader economic factors but simply focus on the labor market and unemployment in each country to determine the importance of a potential skills gap.

In the ManpowerGroup's survey of 40,000 employers in 42 countries the percentage of corporations reporting problems in filling jobs was 40 percent in 2006 and dropped to 35 percent in 2013.[20] Japan had the most difficulty filling jobs in 2013, with 85 percent of surveyed companies reporting problems finding workers, followed by Brazil with 68 percent. At the bottom of the list were South Africa (6 percent), Spain (3 percent) and Ireland (3 percent). Were these problems caused by a skills gap or economic conditions?

The low percentages of employers having problems finding workers in South Africa, Spain, and Ireland are a result of high unemployment making available a large labor pool for employers. The National Bureau of Economic Research reported a South African unemployment rate of 26 percent in 2007.[21] The stated reason for a high unemployment rate was a decline of low-skilled jobs in the mining and agricultural sectors combined with new job market entrants being largely unskilled. The authors noted, "The shrinking demand for and huge influx of relatively unskilled labor created a 'perfect storm', and unemployment among the less-skilled and/or less-experienced workers ballooned . . . High-skilled workers have seen their employment share and their real wages increase as industries, and the economy as a whole, shift towards more skilled workers."[22]

Unlike South Africa, Spain's high unemployment rate is not linked to a lack of skilled workers but a loss of jobs. The International Monetary Fund reported an unemployment rate in Spain of 26 percent in 2014. Spain represents a very complicated situation with 260,000 workers leaving Spain in 2013 with many going to more prosperous countries within the European Union. The actual causes of unemployment are related to a decline in manufacturing jobs (6,000), service sector jobs (109,100), and construction jobs (35,200).[23]

In Ireland, short-term unemployment dropped to 11.8 percent in 2014, but long-term unemployment, defined as collecting unemployment benefits for over 12 months, was 179,335 people or 45.8 percent of total claiming unemployment benefits. One reason for a decline in unemployment in 2014 was, similar to Spain, a result of emigration of unemployed to other countries.[24] Like Spain, the major cause of unemployment was a decline in the number of jobs.

According to Richard Bruton, the Irish government's employment minister, "the building sector had gone from accounting for roughly 17 per cent of Irish gross domestic product in 2006 to 5 per cent now. Some two-thirds of the industry workforce from the peak years, or about 100,000 people, were now unemployed."[25]

In summary, those countries reporting the fewest problems filling jobs had high unemployment rates resulting from a loss of jobs. In South Africa, the loss of jobs in mining and agriculture was accompanied by a high number of unskilled laborers, while Spain and Ireland job loss was accompanied by emigration to other countries. Only in South Africa could one claim that a skills gap was contributing to unemployment.

In Japan, with the highest percentage of companies reporting difficulty in filling jobs, the problem was a labor shortage and not a skills gap. According to Reuters, "Japanese employers were offering 109 jobs for every 100 job seekers in May, the 18th consecutive rise in the ratio, government data show. Job advertisements were up sharply in manufacturing and services."[26] The causes of the labor shortage were immigration laws limiting the number of foreign workers and population decline.[27]

Brazil, the second country listed by ManpowerGroup as having the most difficulty filling jobs, has a very low unemployment rate making it difficult for companies to find workers. Like Japan, Brazil is facing a shrinking labor supply. Writing for *Forbes* magazine, Kenneth Rapoza asserts:

> The decline in [the Brazilian] labor force was driven by a drop in the employed population—now flat in annual terms—as well as by a 3.9% decrease in unemployed people (–11.6% yearly). This combination drove the participation rate down to 55.9% from 56.1% in February, the lowest level since 2002 and well below the historical average of 56.8%.

It reinforces a recent trend in the Brazilian labor market, notes Barclays Capital economist Marcelo Salomon: the decline in the unemployment rate has been supported by fewer people looking for jobs.[28]

Writing for Reuters, Silvio Cascione argues that one reason for the small labor pool is the number of youth returning to schools or other institutions for more skill training: "A key reason why the unemployment rate has remained so low despite weak economic growth is that an increasing number of teenagers and young adults have opted out of the labor force to dedicate more time to training."[29]

In conclusion, the report by the ManpowerGroup of countries with businesses having the most and least difficulty in finding workers illustrates the importance of labor market factors other than the skills gap in achieving economic growth and enhancing corporate earnings. Also, something that I have not discussed is the impact of world economic conditions, particularly the 2008 recession. Except for South Africa, the countries under consideration are experiencing employment problems because of labor shortages and lack of jobs. Japan's labor shortages are related to a low birth rate and national laws making it difficult to bring in foreign workers, while Brazil has low unemployment and many youth out of the labor market training in schools. Spain and Ireland simply lack jobs to ensure full employment while many of their skilled workers head to other countries for employment.

Making Skills-Based Instruction Central to the Curriculum: The Case of Poland

Poland provides an example of how business, despite high unemployment and a large labor pool, can promote a skills-based education. In 2014, the World Bank reported: "Unemployment in Poland is about 14 percent; nearly 25 percent among young workers. High unemployment rates and lack of opportunities lead to difficult living conditions and poverty, with some opting to look for jobs outside the country."[30] Similar to Ireland, many Polish people are emigrating to more prosperous countries. According to the World Bank: "Almost two million Poles reside abroad for more than three months each year, with about two-thirds living outside the country for more than a year, according to the Poland Statistical Office. Most emigrants are younger than 35, and many come from four of the poorest eastern regions in Poland."[31] The ManpowerGroup lists Poland in the bottom half of those countries having difficulty filling jobs with 32 percent of companies reporting this as a problem.[32]

Despite this large labor pool and relatively few companies finding it difficult to fill jobs, the Polish Confederation of Private Employers Lewiatan, which includes 3,500 companies employing over 650,000 workers, is working with the World Economic Federation's project "Repository of Talent Mobility Good Practices" to pressure the national school system to align its curricula with the skill needs of Polish businesses. The Confederation asserted: "that notwithstanding the high unemployment rate, companies have great difficulties in finding the right employees. This is due to the fact that job seekers, the unemployed and graduates from schools and universities are insufficiently qualified."[33]

What this business organization asserts is that Polish businesses "should be involved in shaping curricula."[34] The Confederation surveyed employers and created a skills list for prospective employees. They shared it with educational institutions and announced "that it was promoting educational courses that are in line with employers' needs with special consideration to vocational education. The project formally defined the nature of the skills gap and the pressing need for collaborative solutions."[35]

Poland demonstrates how business in cooperation with the World Economic Forum can implement skills-based educational policies to meet employers' needs. Business takeover of education can result, as suggested earlier, in the undermining of traditional subjects and leave students with employment skills but no knowledge about how the social, political, and economic system works.

The World Economic Forum: Teaching Skills and Linking Schools and Businesses

The World Economic Forum represents global corporations with its membership of "1,000 of the world's top corporations, global enterprises usually with more than US$ 5 billion in turnover." Not surprisingly as a representative of global corporations, the World Economic Forum policy papers strongly support skills-based education.[36] The World Economic Forum sponsors, along with the European Union, "The Qualifications Adjusted to Employers' Needs Project" which "promotes cooperation between the business and education sectors." The goal of the project is "to match, strengthen and develop education programmes in response to labour market changes and employer needs."[37]

In the World Economic Forum's "Issue Overview," discussion of the skills gap reflects the influence of human capital economists discussed in Chapter 1: "Innovation is key for economic growth. Development of human capital is an indispensable driver of an economy's innovative capacity."[38] "Innovation" refers to entrepreneurship education, which I will discuss later in this chapter. In claiming the importance of the skill gap, the World Economic Forum recognized global unemployment problems resulting from the 2008 economic crisis, but declared: "From the perspective of business, neither the high unemployment nor the current crisis has mitigated the urgency of addressing the skills gap issue. The problem of talent shortages requires immediate attention and interdisciplinary action as the unprecedented interconnectedness of the global economy requires a global workforce."[39]

Similar to the Polish Confederation of Private Employers, the World Economic Forum's official position is that government education policies should be synchronized with business needs.

Education: There is insufficient feedback on the effectiveness of education systems and of communication between business and education. Business takes a short-term perspective, education a long-term perspective, while governments focus on the next election. These perspectives must be synchronized to address the skills gap.[40]

As part of the key deficiencies listed by the World Economic Forum in meeting the problem of the skills gap is the "Disconnect between education institutions, business and government: This is reflected in the mismatch between what people learn in school (from early education up to university) and what the market requires."[41]

Not surprisingly, as an organization of global businesses, the World Economic Forum wants worldwide regulation of "talent migration" as part of controlling the skills gap. The reader is reminded of the previous discussions of workers leaving Spain, Ireland, and Poland in search of work in other countries. The World Economic Forum states as a key deficiency international cooperation regarding the skills gap and complains: "No global regulation of talent migration: No global mechanism regulating talent mobility exists, excepting bilateral agreements and a few regional agreements addressing the issue on a fragmentary basis. Best standards are not universally applied."[42] In this context, the World Economic Forum would like international policies to encourage workers to return to their home countries: "Brain circulation: While some developing countries are affected by the brain drain, brain circulation through the return of experienced talent to their home countries, whether temporary or long term, must be encouraged and fostered."[43]

The organization's 2014 report, "Education and Skills 2.0: New Targets and Innovative Approaches," outlines its general policies to help businesses recruit workers with the skills needed for the job. This report represents a major global effort by businesses to ensure that educational systems provide skills-based instruction. The report is a product of collaborative work between World Economic Forum leaders and some Global Agenda Councils, including the Global Agenda Councils of Africa, Pakistan, and Japan, as well as the Council on Youth Unemployment and the Council on Population Growth.[44] The World Economic Forum describes these Global Agenda Councils:

The Network of Global Agenda Councils is a unique, global community of over 1,500 premier thought leaders who are the foremost experts in their fields of academia, business, government, international organizations and society. Grouped in over 80 Councils, Global Agenda Council Members commit their extensive knowledge, expertise and passion to jointly shape the global, regional and industry agenda. The Global Agenda Councils are committed to addressing the most pressing issues and opportunities of our time and aim to provide new thinking and solutions.[45]

"Education and Skills 2.0: New Targets and Innovative Approaches" declares, "policy-makers look for ways to make their economies more competitive in today's fast changing world, a critical factor will be the extent and quality of *education and skills training available for their populations* [author's emphasis]."[46] The report cites a study that found that, in developing countries, between 10 and 20 percent of graduate students are employable by international standards (these standards are never defined). In India, multinational corporations consider only 25 percent of graduate students employable and in Russia 20 percent.[47]

The report is filled with dire warnings, particularly for developing nations, for those failing to link schooling with job skills: "increasingly focus[ing] on the quantity and quality of basic skills, qualified graduate manpower and the lack of expertise in research and development."[48] And the report claims that "by the end of the decade, as research by the McKinsey Global Institute suggests, we will at once be faced with a shortfall of up to 40 million high-skilled workers and a surplus of up to 95 million low-skilled workers."[49]

What is the report's answer to these doomsday findings and predictions? Similar to previously mentioned policy statements, this report advocates a working relationship between educational institutions and employers in what they call "The Education–Skills Nexus."

> Employers, workers and society at large would also be well served by the active use of (possibly new) communication channels among prospective employees, businesses, educators and trainers to promote effectiveness in skills development and job-matching.[50]

In Chapter 5, I will explore in more depth the World Economic Forum's push for partnerships between business, government and civil society. Politically, this is an important issue for education.

Should education policy be primarily influenced by global businesses? On the one hand, this could result, at least according to the World Economic Forum, in low unemployment rates and economic growth. On the other hand, some might argue that skills-based schooling linked to business needs will not prepare students to understand or how to protect their own interests against corporate exploitation. Not surprisingly given its membership, the World Economic Forum presents a benign view of global corporations and its reports suggest that what is good for global corporations is good for all citizens. There is never a hint in their reports that some corporations might be causing environmental degradation, placing profits over employee welfare, and benefiting from their influence on national tax structures. Skills-based education will not prepare workers for these scenarios. Education and Skills 2.0: New Targets and Innovative Approaches urges holding governments accountable for employment rates. It states, "One arena in which accountability matters hugely is the effort to ensure that the skills imparted by an education system match those needed by employers."[51] There is no suggestion that governments hold businesses accountable for economic conditions.

World Economic Forum: Entrepreneurship Education

The World Economic Forum supports entrepreneurial education as part of a skills-based education agenda. Entrepreneurial skills, the organization claims, will stimulate the creation of new companies and help corporate workers think "out of the box." This adds another dimension to the corporatization of human personality. The World Economic Forum's report, "Educating the Next Wave of Entrepreneurs," claims, in a manner similar to others claiming that skills-based education will lead to economic growth, that: "Entrepreneurship is a global phenomenon. The future, to an even greater degree than in the past, will be driven by innovation and entrepreneurship. It is time to more adequately develop entrepreneurial skills, attitudes and behaviors in our schools systems as well as outside formal schools systems, to reach across all ages as part of a lifelong learning process."[52]

The World Economic Forum considers entrepreneurship education as necessary for economic growth. The previously mentioned members of the Global Education Initiative steering committee signed a statement that: "We also believe that entrepreneurship results in increased innovation and sustained economic growth."[53]

The hard and soft skills associated with entrepreneurship education include, "creativity, new venture creation, business idea development and opportunity recognition, business planning, leadership, entrepreneurial marketing, entrepreneurial finance and growth management as well as soft skills like negotiation or presentation competences."[54]

The World Economic Forum recommends that entrepreneurial education be a required course in colleges and universities. Combined with other skill instruction in academic institutions, entrepreneurial education is claimed to be a major contributor to economic growth. The Global Education Initiative on entrepreneurship education aims to: "Encourage all faculties/disciplines to develop opportunities for students at every level to experience entrepreneurship. Integrate entrepreneurship into the curriculum and build towards a multidisciplinary learning environment." The World Economic Forum recommends that academic institutions:

- Increase the number of schools offering entrepreneurship courses, programmes and activities
- Augment the number of entrepreneurship courses, programmes and activities and make them available to a broader group of students
- Make entrepreneurship a required course

- Integrate entrepreneurship across other disciplines
- Encourage entrepreneurship across disciplines, particularly in science and technology.[55]

Also, emphasizing the need for academic institutions to offer courses in entrepreneurship education, the European Roundtable on Entrepreneurship Education issued a "Manifesto" which declares: "Governments across Europe must act to address the growing skills gap."[56] Similar to the previously stated skills associated with entrepreneurship education, the Manifesto declares that educational institutions need to develop programs that provide the "appropriate learning environment for encouraging creativity, innovation and the ability to think 'out of the box' to solve problems." The Manifesto urges: "Academic institutions in Europe must revamp their programmes to enable the development of 21st century skills."[57]

In combination with teaching skills for employment, the entrepreneurial skills are supposed to stimulate economic growth and create jobs.[58] In the vision of those promoting entrepreneurial education, these economic benefits will result from people starting new businesses and creating new jobs.

OECD and Skills Instruction

OECD is a major global proponent of skills-based education and is providing tests for measuring skills. OECD has a dedicated skills website (http://skills.oecd.org/) which carries the hopeful logo "OECD: Better Policies for Better Lives."[59] A diagram on its website declares: "Building the right skills can help countries improve economic prosperity and social cohesion."[60] The diagram portrays teaching the right skills as contributing to health, civil, and social engagement plus improvement in productivity, economic growth, high levels of employment, and good quality jobs. A diagram arrow labeled "How is this achieved?" points to the answer, "By strengthening skills systems."[61] OECD advocates designing a national skills strategy, funding skills instruction, and providing information to companies and the public about the importance of skills instruction.

Skills are supposed to be the magic bullet for solving both economic and social problems. In an early twenty-first-century publication, *The Well-being of Nations: The Role of Human and Social Capital Education and Skills*, OECD writers list what they consider to be key skills: "Communication: listening, speaking, reading, or writing" and "Numeracy."[62] In addition, the OECD document promotes soft skills, such as "Intrapersonal skills: motivation/perseverance, learning to learn, and capacity to make judgments" and "Interpersonal skills: teamwork and leadership."[63] Consequently, the educational emphasis is on teaching literacy (reading, writing, and oral expression) and mathematics (numeracy). Soft skills are to be taught in preschool, throughout other years of schooling, in the family, and in the child's social relationships.

OECD: Survey of Adult Skills (PIAAC)

OECD measures adult skills in OECD countries through the Programme for the International Assessment of Adult Competencies (PIAAC).[64] In administering PIAAC, OECD identifies the key skills for a modern technologically driven global economy as: "proficiency in literacy, numeracy and problem solving in technology-rich environments—the key information-processing skills that are invaluable in 21st-century economies—and in various "generic" skills, such as co-operation, communication, and organizing one's time."[65] These skills are described as providing a "foundation for effective and successful participation in the social and economic life of advanced economies."[66]

OECD's 2013 report of PIAAC surveys and testing reveals that most nations have adopted a skills approach to education: "One of the explicit goals of the school systems in the countries that participated in the Survey of Adult Skills is to ensure that students leave compulsory education with adequate *literacy and numeracy skills and with the ability to use information and communication technologies; and this continues to be a goal at higher levels of education too* [author's emphasis].[67]

From a sociological perspective, PIAAC's 2013 report on socio-demographic distribution of skills is not surprising. Similar to early human capital studies discussed in Chapter 1 that found a relationship between educational attainment and family income, the report states that adults from "socio-economically advantaged backgrounds" have higher average scores in literacy, numeracy, and problem solving in technological-rich environments than those not from advantaged backgrounds and that adults who attend higher education institutions have higher literacy scores than those who don't.[68] Those with at least one parent who attained a higher education degree have higher literacy and numeracy scores than those who do not have one parent with a higher education degree. Those with the lowest attained skills had the lowest paying jobs. In other words, if you were born into a socio-economically advantaged family you are more likely to attain the skills needed for higher paying jobs.

Does everyone need to attain high levels of these specified skills, since there continue to be many occupations requiring low levels of educational attainment? One answer given in the PIAAC report is that equalizing skill levels will decrease inequalities in income and provide for economic mobility out of poverty. But someone stills needs to do work, particularly in the service industry, which only requires low levels of educational attainment. The PIAAC report justifies skills training for workers in jobs requiring a low level of educational attainment to prepare them for the introduction of new technology.

Also, the PIAAC report shows a decline of low-skilled jobs in OECD countries because these jobs are being outsourced to developing nations. The PIAAC survey states: "Globalisation has also led to the outsourcing of production. Low-skilled jobs are increasingly seen as being 'offshoreable'—i.e. being relocated from high wage or high cost locations to low wage and low cost locations in less developed countries."[69]

The PIAAC survey provides a variety of differing soft skills needed for employment, sometimes calling soft skills 'generic' skills: "In addition to mastering occupation-specific skills, workers in the 21st century must also have . . . 'generic' skills, such as interpersonal communication, self-management, and the ability to learn, to help them weather the uncertainties of a rapidly changing labour market."[70] Citing a World Bank study, the OECD asserts "conscientiousness" as a factor in educational attainment.

> Socio-emotional skills are correlated with educational attainment. In all . . . countries, greater openness and higher levels of conscientiousness are correlated with a higher level of education; neuroticism seems negatively correlated. Extraversion and agreeableness are not significantly correlated with education.[71]

As I discuss later, conscientiousness is considered by some economists as a key soft skill for educational attainment and higher incomes.

The PIAAC report's data on the relationship between skills and "well-being," introduces another set of soft skills called the four dimensions of well-being: "the level of trust in others; political efficacy or the sense of influence on the political process; participation in associative, religious, political or charity activities (volunteering); and self-assessed health status."[72]

What is interesting about the soft skills related to well-being, in contrast to soft skills needed for work, is that they include a measure of a person's trust in business. The PIAAC survey asserts: "Trust is the bedrock of democracy. Without trust in others and in the rule of law, all relationships, whether business, political or social, function less efficiently."[73] Should a person trust business organizations? If the primary goal of business is to make money using advertising, do we really want consumers to trust advertising messages? Does business work in the interests of the consumer? Should we trust government and the rule of law? A potential of teaching "trust" might be a reduction of critical thinking about money and power as related to global corporations and national governments.

Undoubtedly, PIAAC will be used by national education policy leaders to justify a skills-based curriculum for their schools. As reflected in the previous discussion of trust as a factor in well-being, there is no suggestion of providing the skills to critically think about the actions of corporations or governments. PIAAC serves the interests of global corporations in providing educated workers who will be proficient in literacy, numeracy, and problem solving in technology-rich environments. Once hired, it is hoped, they will have the soft skills of cooperation, communication, and being able to organize their work time.

The World Bank's Step Skills Measurement Program: Shaping the Corporate Personality

The World Bank, as I discuss in more detail in Chapter 6, has played a major role in the economization of education in developing countries. Similar to OECD, the World Bank has developed a skills measurement protocol using the same scale as OECD's PIAAC. This scale includes ideal personality attributes for economic success.

Similar to other groups discussed in this chapter, the World Bank's publication, *Learning for All Investing in People's Knowledge and Skills to Promote Development: World Bank Group Education Strategy 2020,* declares: "Persistently high levels of unemployment, especially among youth, have highlighted the failure of education systems to prepare young people with the right skills for the job market and have fueled calls for greater opportunity and accountability."[74] The World Bank publication warns that a school diploma may increase individual employability but it does not necessarily reflect a worker's skills that would contribute to increased productivity and economic growth. It claims that: "Recent research shows that the level of skills in a workforce predicts economic growth rates far better than do average schooling levels."[75]

To implement its 2020 strategy, the World Bank Group will focus on "knowledge generation and exchange" along with technical and financial support and cooperation with other groups. Assessment of the educational system is considered key to ensuring the teaching of the right skills which include basic competencies of reading and numeracy, critical thinking, problem solving, and team skills.[76]

The World Bank's "Step Skills Measurement Program" is designed to measure hard and soft skills and it collected from 2012 to 2014 measurement data from urban adults aged 15 to 64 in Armenia, Bolivia, Colombia, Georgia, Ghana, Lao PDR, Sri Lanka, Vietnam, and the Yunnan Province in China.[77] The Step assessment includes a household survey of work-related skills, educational attainment, job training, health, and employment history.

An important aspect of these household surveys is their targeting of personality characteristics, which as I discuss in Chapter 6, has become part of the economization argument, particularly regarding preschool education. The family is considered important for developing the right soft skills and as preparation for learning hard skills in school. This economic approach to family life is reflected in the three modules of the household survey, namely:

- **a direct assessment of reading proficiency** and related competencies scored on the same scale as the OECD's PIAAC (International Assessment of Adult Competencies);
- self-reported information on **personality, behavior, and time and risk preferences** (e.g., Big Five, Grit, decision-making, and hostile attribution bias); and
- **job-relevant skills** that respondents possess or use in their job.[78]

Of particular interest in this World Bank survey is the concern with personality and behavior or the soft skills needed for corporate life. This has implications for both restructuring family life and using education to develop soft skills considered necessary for the operation of global businesses. This involves the economization of personalities and households to ensure productive work within global corporations.

The STEP household survey refers, as stated above, to "Big Five, Grit, decision-making and hostile attribution bias." In my research, the closest proposal I have found for developing similar character attributes is in the work of Nobel Laureate and University of Chicago economist James Heckman. He argues, as I discuss in Chapter 6, that families should develop certain soft skills needed for economic success, specifically "Grit, Perseverance, Delay of gratification, Impulse control, Achievement striving, Ambition, and Work ethic."[79] The reliance on Heckman's argument is stated clearly in the 2014 publication "STEP Skills Measurement Surveys Innovative Tools for Assessing Skills."

> Research by James Heckman and other economists in OECD countries in the past 15 years has conclusively demonstrated the importance of personality traits—such as conscientiousness, persistence, work motivation, extraversion, emotional resilience, ability to work with others, and willingness to bear risk—in determining labor market and other educational outcomes over an individual's lifetime."[80]

The reference to the "Big Five" in the three survey modules refers to conscientiousness, openness to experience, neuroticism, agreeableness, and extraversion.[81] The definition of conscientiousness shows its potential importance for employers: "the propensity to follow socially prescribed norms for impulse control, to be goal directed, to plan, and to be able to delay gratification and to follow norms and rules."[82] This attribute is measured by the following questions in the STEP Skills Household Survey: "When doing a task, are you very careful?"[83]

Other questions asked in the household survey for particular attributes are:

- Openness to experience refers to enjoyment of learning and new ideas: "Do you come up with ideas other people haven't thought of before?"
- Neuroticism refers to the tendency to feel negative emotions: "Do you worry a lot?"
- Agreeableness refers to a pro-social, cooperative orientation to others: "Do you forgive other people easily?"
- Extraversion encompasses sociability and dominance in social situations: "Are you talkative?"[84]

"Grit" in the survey is defined as perseverance in achieving long-term goals. The STEP survey includes three questions to measure grit:

- Do you finish whatever you begin?
- Do you work very hard? For example, do you keep working when others stop to take a break?
- Do you enjoy working on things that take a very long time (at least several months) to complete?[85]

Questions for "Decision-making" are:

- Do you think about how the things you do will affect you in the future?
- Do you think carefully before you make an important decision?
- Do you ask for help when you don't understand something?
- Do you think about how the things you will do will affect others?"[86]
  "Hostile Attribution Bias" questions are:
- Do people take advantage of you?
- Are people mean/not nice to you?[87]

The World Bank's Step Skills Measurement Program provides a skills assessment for developing countries similar to OECD's PIAAC for developed countries. These two assessment programs create world standards for measuring skills wanted and/or needed by global corporations. An important dimension of the World Bank's assessment is its measurement of personality characteristics wanted by global businesses. As I discuss in Chapter 6, there are some important cultural dimensions to these personality characteristics that are in conflict with character traits of other cultures. I would argue that the traits measured by the Step Skills Measurement Program provide an outline of a global personality and one that may dominate the world as globalization progresses.

An Example of Educating for Corporate Skills: Common Core State Standards

The World Economic Forum, OECD, and the World Bank's categorization of skills is reflected in the policies of member nations. An example of the corporatization of the curriculum is the US interpretation of literacy as a skill needed by the global economy. Forty-five states in the United States (as of 2014) adopted what are called Common Core State Standards in the areas identified by OECD, namely literacy (English Language Arts) and Mathematics. Like OECD, the Common Core State Standards, as mentioned earlier, are designed to increase economic growth and productivity.[i]

---

i The Mission Statement of the Common Core State Curriculum claims: "With American students fully prepared for the future, our communities will be best positioned to compete successfully in the global economy." Common Core State Standards, "Mission." Retrieved from http://www.corestandards.org/ on February 26, 2014.

The Common Core State Standards for English Language Arts parallel the skills listed in the previously discussed documents: reading, writing, speaking and listening, language [vocabulary], and media and technology.[88]

In the American context, literacy standards are directly linked to the needs of corporations. David Coleman, an architect of the Common Core Standards and president of the College Board, explained his push for students to write fewer personal and opinion pieces. As reported by Tamar Lewin in the *New York Times*, he asserted that in the working world a person would not say: "Johnson, I need a market analysis by Friday, but before that I need a compelling account of your childhood."[89]

As reported by Catherine Gewertz in *Education Week*, David Liben, a former New York City teacher and now a senior literacy specialist with Student Achievement Partners, a group founded to promote the Common Core State Standards by David Coleman, Susan Pimentel, and Jason Zimba, who were also lead writers of the Standards,[90] told teachers that the Common Core literacy standards "virtually eliminate[s] text-to-self connections."[91] Liben directed teachers to eliminate from basal readers any questions dealing with how students feel about a reading along with any questions asking about the meaning of the reading in the students' life. "In college and careers, no one cares how you feel," Mr. Liben said. "Imagine being asked to write a memo on why your company's stock price has plummeted: 'Analyze why and tell me how you feel about it'."[92]

In this context, literacy becomes a tool for employment not cultural enrichment, entertainment, or personal understanding. Knowledge of traditional subjects, as I discussed previously, becomes a vehicle for learning employment skills. This argument is reinforced by the official Common Core State Standards Initiative's answer to the question: "Do the Common Core State Standards incorporate both content and skills?" The answer is "Yes" but the only content specified is in literacy and math standards. Content specified for literacy standards is:

- Classic myths and stories from around the world
- America's founding documents
- Foundational American literature
- Shakespeare.[93]

For math, the specified content is:

- Whole numbers
- Addition
- Subtraction
- Multiplication
- Division
- Fractions
- Decimals.[94]

While this specified content might prepare students for math and nationalistic feelings through exploring "America's founding documents" and "Foundational American literature," Anglo-Saxon cultural traditions through teaching "Shakespeare," and a brief glimpse of global culture through teaching "Classic myths and stories from around the world," there is no specified content that would help the student understand global political, social, and economic conditions. The specified content might prepare future workers, but it does not prepare students for acting to improve their life conditions and those of the world.

Is there a skills gap that the Common Core State Standards attempts to address? Is there a global skills gap that is causing unemployment and inequality of incomes and hurting economic growth? Are these changes in curricula justified by the so-called skills gap?

The Skills Gap

Princeton economist, Nobel Prize winner, and *New York Times* columnist Paul Krugman is an important critic of the argument that a skills gap is hurting national economies. He argues that in the 2014 US economy there are three times more unemployed than jobs available.[95] This situation parallels my previous discussion of conditions in Ireland and Spain. Krugman calls the skills gap a zombie idea because no matter how much the idea is disproved it continues to exist. Krugman claims "multiple careful studies have found no support for claims that inadequate worker skills explain high unemployment."[96]

Krugman argues that workers with more education have always had lower unemployment rates and that in 2014 unemployment across the skills spectrum resulted from the financial crisis of 2007. One of the studies he uses to support his argument was conducted by the Boston Consulting Group (BCG) which has 80 offices around the world. Their report, "Skills Gap in U.S. Manufacturing is Less Pervasive than Many Believe," concluded that "findings underscore the idea that worries of a skills gap crisis are overblown. Thirty-seven percent of respondents whose companies had shifted manufacturing to the U.S. from another country cited 'better access to skilled workforce or talent' as a strong factor in their decision. Only 8 percent, one-fifth as many, cited this as a reason for moving production out of the U.S."[97]

Krugman's criticism of the continuing myth of a skills mismatch is supported by a US Federal Reserve article published in 2012 titled "Is there a skills mismatch in the labor market?"[98] After reviewing a number of studies, the article concludes that since the 2007 recession there is mixed evidence of a skill mismatch. Their review of the supply and demand of workers according to skill levels found "limited evidence of skills mismatch." The one group that might be experiencing a mismatch, the article claims, are those with a "moderate amount of skills . . . If there is a skills mismatch in the U.S. labor market, therefore, it may be most significant for this group."[99]

Why the continued claim of a skills gap? Krugman answers that it is because leaders are unwilling to change fiscal policies that undermine employment and wages. More importantly, he claims it shifts the burden of responsibility to the worker:

> Moreover, by blaming workers for their own plight, the skills myth shifts attention away from the spectacle of soaring profits and bonuses even as employment and wages stagnate. Of course, that may be another reason corporate executives like the myth so much.[100]

In a similar critique, economist Andrew Hacker challenges the projections made by Anthony P. Carnevale, Nicole Smith, and Jeff Strohl in their book *Share Help Wanted: Projections of Jobs and Education Requirements Through 2018*. According to Hacker, the book claims the US economy: "will 'need 22 million new college degrees,' that is, many of the jobs available will require college degrees" and "the economy 'will fall short of that number by at least 3 million.' (At another point, they propose a 'goal of producing 8.2 million new college graduates.')"[101] The argument that the economy will need more college graduates has been one of the justifications for the Common Core State Standards. Hacker also questions the idea that students need more math because, he argues, "In fact, relatively few jobs require using mathematics—algebra, calculus, or trigonometry—for working tasks."[102]

Hacker's arguments are supported by the occupation projections of the US Bureau of Labor Statistics. In 2012, in the midst of the implementation of the Common Core State Standards, the Bureau's statistical report on occupations declared, "The most new jobs from 2012 to 2022 are projected to be in occupations that typically can be entered with a high school diploma."[103] Also, the statistics revealed that there would be more jobs for those with less than a high school diploma than for those with Bachelor's degrees. The job projections show the number of occupations requiring a high school diploma or its equivalent will grow by 4,630,800 and those occupations requiring less than a high school diploma will increase by 4,158,400. In contrast, the projections show that jobs for those with Bachelor's degrees will increase by 3,143,600, while those for occupations requiring a Doctoral or professional degree will rise by 638,400, Master's degree by 448,500, Associate's degree by 1,046,000, and some college, no degree by 225,000.[104]

The US Bureau of Labor Statistics report claims that 91 percent of workers entering jobs requiring only a high school diploma will be trained on the job. Forty-five percent of these workers with only high school diplomas will enter apprenticeship programs, while 13 percent will receive long-term on-the-job training for more than 12 months, 4 percent would have one month to a year of on-the-job training, and 9 percent less than one month. The remaining workers with only a high school diploma will not receive on-the-job training.[105]

The report states, "Apprenticeship occupations are projected to grow the fastest during the 2012-22 decade."[106] Many of these apprenticeship programs will be in the construction industry.

In agreement with the early human capitalist economists discussed in Chapter 1, the Bureau of Labor Statistics found income paralleling educational credentials with those with a high school diploma having an average wage of $35,170 in contrast to those with Associate's degree ($57,590), Bachelor's degree ($67,140) and Doctoral or professional degree ($96,420). There were some anomalies in these income statistics. For instance, those with some college, no degree ($28,730) and post-secondary non-degree award ($34,760) will earn less than the $35,170 for those with only high school diplomas. Also, those with Master's degrees ($63,400) will earn less than those with Bachelor's degrees ($67,140).[107]

Conclusion

Is a skills-based curriculum educating workers to meet corporate employment needs but leaving them without the knowledge and tools to protect their economic and political rights? The OECD, the World Bank, and the World Economic Forum are promoting skills-based curricula to meet the employment needs of corporations. As detailed in Chapter 1, human capital economists in the 1950s and 1960s began to emphasize skills learned in school for economic success in contrast to actual subjects. By the twenty-first century this resulted in a call for skills-based curricula in which content knowledge in literacy and math is considered important but not the content of other subjects. Other subjects become important for teaching skills related to information processing and reasoning.

The drive for skills-based curricula includes soft skills designed to create a corporate personality to meet the organizational needs of global businesses. Besides denuding curricula of subjects and topics that might help citizens protect their economic and political rights, surveys of global corporations show a desire for worker characteristics that are stripped of concerns about social justice and protection of human and environmental rights. These soft skills include, as embodied in the World Bank's Step Skills Measurement Program, "Grit, Perseverance, Delay of gratification, Impulse control, Achievement striving, Ambition, and Work ethic." There is also a desire by companies for employees who are able to work in teams and have a sense of trust towards governments and business activities.

The result of skills-based curricula might be compliant corporate employees who do not question internal business orders or act to protect their own economic rights. Certainly, there is no stated objective in proposed skills-based schooling to teach students how governments might regulate business activities to ensure fairness to consumers or protect workers from economic exploitation or dictatorial political actions.

Simply stated, skills-based learning educates a cog to fit into corporate machinery to ensure increased profits. Even traditional liberal arts curricula are being tossed aside as corporations try to align school instruction with their needs. The argument that economic problems are caused by a skills gap leads to the suggestion of a closer alliance between businesses and public schooling. Should schooling primarily serve the interests of business? Is the growing economization of education leading to national oligarchies dominated by business interests? What happened to ideas about educating for democratic citizenship and social justice?

Notes

1 OECD, *Trends Shaping Education 2013 (Paris: OECD Publishing 2013), p. 11.*

2 Seán Ó Riain, "Human Capital Formation Regimes: States, Markets, and Human Capital in an Era of Globalization" in *The Oxford Handbook of Human Capital* edited by Alan Burton-Jones and J. C. Spender (Oxford: Oxford University Press, 2011), p. 589.

3 Ibid.

4 Ibid.

5 OECD Center for Educational Research and Innovation, *The Well-being of Nations: The Role of Human and Social Capital Education and Skills* (Paris: OECD, 2001), p. 18.

6 World Economic Forum, "Education and Skills 2.0: New Targets and Innovative Approaches" (Geneva: World Economic Forum, January 2014), p. 13.

7 National Association of Colleges and Employers, "The Job Outlook for the Class of 2014." Retrieved from http://www.naceweb.org/uploadedFiles/Pages/MyNACE/grab_and_go/students/job-outlook-2014-student-version.pdf on February 15, 2014.

8 Ibid.

9 Ibid.

10 Adecco, "About Us." Retrieved from http://www.adeccousa.com/about/Pages/welcome.aspx on February 17, 2014.

11 Adecco, "The Skills Gap and the State of the Economy." Retrieved from http://www.slideshare.net/AdeccoUSA/adecco-state-of-the-economy-survey-media-deck-final on February 17, 2014.

12 OECD Center for Educational Research and Innovation, *The Well-being of Nations . . .*, p. 19.

13 The ManpowerGroup, "2013 Talent Shortage Survey," p. 2. Retrieved from http://www.manpowergroup.us/campaigns/talent-shortage-2013/ on February 17, 2014.

14 ManpowerGroup, "About." Retrieved from http://www.manpowergroup.com/wps/wcm/connect/manpowergroup-en/home/about on February 17, 2014.

15 The ManpowerGroup, "2013 Talent Shortage Survey," p. 8.

16 Ibid., p. 8.

17 Scott Jaschik, "Disappearing Liberal Arts Colleges," INSIDE HIGHER ED (October 11, 2012). Retrieved from http://www.insidehighered.com/news/2012/10/11/study-finds-liberal-arts-colleges-are-disappearing#sthash.aiQ50mpT.dpbs on July 17, 2014.

18 The City University of New York, "Pathways FAQs" (April 8, 2013). Retrieved from http://www1.cuny.edu/mu/academic-news/2013/04/08/pathways-general-education-requirements-at-cuny-qa/ on July 17, 2014.

19 Ibid.

20 The ManpowerGroup, "2013 Talent Shortage Survey," p. 4.

21 Abhijit Banerjee, Sebastian Galiani, Jim Levinsohn, Zoë McLaren, and Ingrid Woolard, "Why Has Unemployment Risen in the New South Africa," National Bureau of Economic Research, NBER Working Paper No. 13167 (June 2007), p. 2. Retrieved from http://www.nber.org/papers/w13167 on July 18, 2014.

22 Ibid., pp. 2–3.

23 Stephen Burgen, "Spain's unemployment rise tempers green shoots of recovery: Despite unemployment falling by 65,000 in 2013, jobless rate now above 26% owing to smaller working age population," *The Guardian* (January 23, 2014). Retrieved from http://www.theguardian.com/world/2014/jan/23/spain-unemployment-rise-26-percent on July 18, 2014.

24 Ciara Kenny, "Unemployment rate falls to 11.8 per cent in March," *Irish Times* (April 2, 2014). Retrieved from http://www.irishtimes.com/business/economy/unemployment-rate-falls-to-11-8-per-cent-in-march-1.1747109 on July 18, 2014.

25 Vincent Boland, "Irish unemployment falls after exit from international bailout," *Financial Times* (February 27, 2014). Retrieved from http://www.ft.com/intl/cms/s/0/44c4578a-9fd6-11e3-9c65-00144feab7de.html#axzz37pkXroks on July 18, 2014.

26 Reuters, "Labor shortage: Japanese firms near crisis point" (July 11, 2014). Retrieved from http://www.arabnews.com/news/600391 on July 18, 2014.

27 Alexandra Harney and Antoni Slodkowski, "Special Report: Foreign interns pay the price for Japan's labor shortage," Reuters (June 12, 2014). Retrieved from http://www.reuters.com/article/2014/06/12/us-japan-labour-special-report-idUSKBN0EN06G20140612 on July 18, 2014.

28 Kenneth Rapoza, "Why Brazil's Unemployment Rate Is So Low," Forbes April 17, 2014. Retrieved from http://www.forbes.com/sites/kenrapoza/2014/04/17/why-brazils-unemployment-rate-is-so-low/ on July 18, 2014.

29 Silvio Cascione, "UPDATE 1-Brazil unemployment under 5 pct despite weak job growth," Reuters (May 22, 2014). Retrieved from http://www.reuters.com/article/2014/05/22/brazil-economy-jobless-idUSL1N0O80GM20140522 on July 18, 2014.

30 The World Bank, "Young, Under-employed, and Poor in Poland" (February 10, 2014). Retrieved from http://www.worldbank.org/en/news/feature/2014/02/10/young-underemployed-and-poor-in-poland on July 22, 2014.

31 Ibid.

32 The ManpowerGroup, "2013 Talent Shortage Survey," p. 5.

33 World Economic Forum, "Repository of Talent mobility Good Practices: Qualifications Adjusted to Employers' Needs Project." Retrieved from http://www.weforum.org/best-practices/talent-mobility/qualifications-adjusted-employers%E2%80%99-needs-project on July 22, 2014.

34 Ibid.

35 Ibid.

36 World Economic Forum, "Members." Retrieved from http://www.weforum.org/our-members on February 20, 2014.

37 Ibid.

38 World Economic Forum, "Skills Gap: Issue Overview" (undated). Retrieved from http://www.weforum.org/pdf/GAC09/council/skills_gap/print_issue.htm on July 24, 2014.

39 Ibid.

40 Ibid.

41 Ibid.

42 Ibid.

43 Ibid.

44 World Economic Forum, "Education and Skills 2.0 . . . ," p. 5.

45 World Economic Forum, "Global Agenda Councils." Retrieved from http://www. weforum.org/community/global-agenda-councils on August 4, 2014.

46 Ibid., p. 4.

47 Ibid., pp. 8–9.

48 Ibid., p. 7

49 Ibid., p. 7.

50 Ibid., p. 10.

51 Ibid., p. 13.

52 Ibid., p. 8.

53 Ibid., p. 6.

54 Ibid., p. 15.

55 Ibid., p. 28.

56 Global Education Initiative, European Roundtable on Entrepreneurship Education, "Manifesto." Retrieved from http://www3.weforum.org/docs/WEF_GEI_ EuropeanRoundtable_Manifesto_2010.pdf on February 24, 2014.

57 Ibid.

58 Ibid.

59 Skills OECD, "Logo." Retrieved from http://skills.oecd.org/ on February 15, 2014.

60 Skills OECD, "Building the right skills." Retrieved from http://skills.oecd.org/ media/skills/oecd-infographics/OECD-infographic-for-print.pdf on February 15, 2014.

61 Ibid.

62 OECD Center for Educational Research and Innovation, *The Well-being of Nations* . . . , p. 19.

63 Ibid.

64 OECD, "OECD Skills Surveys." Retrieved from http://www.oecd.org/site/piaac/ on February 16, 2014.

65 OECD, "OECD Skills Outlook 2013: First Results from the Survey of Adult Skills (2013)," p. 3. Retrieved from http://dx.doi.org/10.1787/9789264204256-en on February 16, 2014.

66 Ibid., p. 52.

67 Ibid., p. 118.

68 Ibid., pp. 104, 114.

69 Ibid., p. 51.

70 Ibid., p. 46.

71 Ibid., p. 236.

72 Ibid., p. 234.

73 Ibid., p. 237.

74 The International Bank for Reconstruction and Development/The World Bank, *Learning for All Investing in People's Knowledge and Skills to Promote Development: World Bank Group Education Strategy 2020 (Washington, DC: The International Bank for Reconstruction and Development/The World Bank, 2011)*, p. v.

75 Ibid., p. 5.

76 Ibid., p. 8.

77 The World Bank, "STEP Skills Measurement Program (STEP)," *Data* (2014) Retrieved from http://microdata.worldbank.org/index.php/catalog/step/about on July 23, 2014.

78 Ibid.

79 James Heckman and Tim D. Kautz, "Hard Evidence on Soft Skills" (Cambridge, MA: National Bureau of Economic Research, 2012), p. 13.

80 Gaëlle Pierre, Maria Laura Sanchez Puerta, Alexandria Valerio, and Tania Rajadel, "STEP Skills Measurement Surveys: Innovative Tools for Assessing Skills July 9, 2014" World Bank, p. 28. Retrieved from http://microdata.worldbank.org/index.php/catalog/2012/download/30679 on July 23, 2014.

81 Ibid., p. 29.

82 Ibid., p. 31.

83 Ibid., p. 31.

84 Ibid., p. 31.

85 Ibid., p. 31.

86 Ibid., p. 78.

87 Ibid., p. 78.

88 Common Core State Standards, "Key Points in English Language Arts." Retrieved from http://www.corestandards.org/resources/key-points-in-english-language-arts on February 15, 2014.

89 Tamar Lewin, "Backer of Common Core School Curriculum Is Chosen to Lead College Board," *New York Times* (May 16, 2012). Retrieved from http://www.nytimes.com/2012/05/16/education/david-coleman-to-lead-college-board.html on March 4, 2013.

90 Achieve the Core, "Our Purpose." Retrieved from http://achievethecore.org/about-us on March 17, 2014.

91 Catherine Gewertz, "Teachers Reflect Standards in Basals," Education Week (May 9, 2012). Retrieved from http://www.edweek.org/ew/articles/2012/04/26/30basal.h31.html?qs=Gewertz May 10, 2012.

92 Ibid.

93 Common Core State Standards Initiative, "Frequently Asked Questions." Retrieved from http://www.corestandards.org/about-the-standards/frequently-asked-questions/ on July 24, 2014.

94 Ibid.

95 Paul Krugman, "Jobs and Skills and Zombies," *The New York Times* (March 30, 2014). Retrieved from http://www.nytimes.com/2014/03/31/opinion/krugman-jobs-and-skills-and-zombies.html?_r=1 on July 18, 2014. He cites the following for his data on unemployed versus jobs: Gene Sperling, "Our economy still has three people looking for every job (opening)," *Tampa Bay Times* (January 5, 2014). Retrieved from http://www.politifact.com/truth-o-meter/statements/2014/jan/07/gene-sperling/there-are-3-unemployed-people-every-job-opening-ob/ on July 23, 2014.

96 Krugman, "Jobs and Skills and Zombies."

97 Boston Consulting Group, "Skills Gap in U.S. Manufacturing Is Less Pervasive than Many Believe" (October 15, 2012). Retrieved from http://www.bcg.com/media/PressReleaseDetails.aspx?id=tcm%3A12-118945 on July 23, 2014.

98 R. Jason Faberman and Bhashkar Mazumder, "Is there a skills mismatch in the labor market?" Essays On Issues. The Federal Reserve Bank Of Chicago (July 2012), Number 300.

99 Ibid., p. 3.

100 Krugman, "Jobs and Skills and Zombies."

101 Andrew Hacker, "Where Will We Find the Jobs? by Andrew Hacker," *The New York Review of Books* (February 24, 2011). Retrieved from http://www.nybooks.com/articles/archives/2011/feb/24/where-will-we-find-jobs/ on July 24, 2014.

102 Ibid.

103 US Bureau of Labor Statistics, "Education and Training outlook for occupations, 2012–22 (2012)," p. 3. Retrieved from http://www.bls.gov/emp/ep_edtrain_outlook.pdf on July 24, 2014.

104 Ibid., p. 3.

105 Ibid., p. 5.

106 Ibid., p. 4.

107 Ibid., p. 6.

4

WORLD BANK

"Our Dream Is a World Free of Poverty"

The World Bank contributes to the economization of education as it focuses on the development of the world's poorest nations. Its education concerns go far beyond preparing a workforce for economic growth. Their interests also include the general welfare of a nation, the quality of life, and the environment. Included in Bank plans are previously discussed ideas, namely human capital, skills, and test scores on TIMSS and PISA. Its economization of education occurred as part of the unfolding of the Bank's developmental philosophy.

Called "the world's most powerful international institution"[1] and "the architect of what has become a truly global education policy,"[2] the Bank lends money and provides technical assistance to "developing" countries and supports education projects to reduce poverty and spur economic growth and stability. During the presidency of Robert McNamara (1968–1981) the Bank took on the task of eliminating world poverty. At the entrance to its Washington, DC building is the motto: "Our Dream Is a World Free of Poverty."[3] World Bank education strategies are dominated by economists. Complaining about the impact of the World Bank on local schools, Gita Steiner-Khamsi writes, "One could simply criticize the World Bank for encouraging economists with doctoral degrees to carry out educational research."[4]

The Bank is a global promoter of human capital education through its e-learning courses in the economics of education. The goal of their e-learning courses is to help educational leaders to: "Use economic tools and concepts such as human capital theory, rate of return, and individual vs. social costs and benefits to make decisions regarding education reform."[5] The course is to help educators think like economists. By the end of the course, students are told that they will:

- Understand economic methods for evaluating education projects such as discounting, cost–benefit analysis, cost–effectiveness analysis, and impact evaluation.

- Identify the factors that influence supply and demand in education, and how government policies affect these factors.
- Explain how markets function using supply and demand analysis.
- Understand the economic dimensions of education production, including education production functions, marginal vs. average productivity, the law of diminishing returns, and economies of scale.
- Present an economic case for a particular education reform.

Currently, World Bank economists, like OECD, utilize concepts of human capital and emphasize skills over years of schooling. It also relies on PISA and TIMSS to measure the impact of educational loans and technical assistance. What is different from OECD is the World Bank's primary concern with development and poverty. Development programs raise a series of questions directly impacting the Bank's education agenda. What is an underdeveloped country? What are the cultural implications of changing underdeveloped countries to developed countries? How do you define poverty? Is the definition of poverty dependent on a particular cultural viewpoint? How do education programs aid development and eliminate poverty while protecting local cultures? Are education programs for development making all countries similar and thus aiding in the creation of a world education culture?

The concern in this chapter is the Bank's contribution to the economization of education. I will not be writing about the protests and general complaints about the Bank's work which have indebted many of the world's poorest nations and peoples while being environmentally destructive. A lot of space could be devoted to this topic, but I am limiting my concerns to the Bank's justifications for investing in education. As an example of problems with its general funding, sociologist Michael Goldman, in his book with the descriptive title *Imperial Nature*, describes a World Bank project in India to irrigate a desert region with water from the Himalayas. In the end, the project benefited wealthy land owners at the expense of poor farmers. Concrete used to line irrigation canals was only poured for those canals near prosperous farms. Project managers and government officials used the concrete designated for canals affecting poorer landowners to build themselves new housing. The result was the rich got richer and the poor were encumbered with high debt.[6]

Given the extent of World Bank activities, my focus on education neglects its full impact on developing nations and the world economy. One basic criticism of its lending policies is the requirement that loan money be used to buy a substantial percentage of goods from the wealthy nations controlling the Bank. For instance, loans for infrastructure projects like power plants and roads resulted in developing countries being in debt to companies in developed countries. The resulting debts to the World Bank and foreign companies give the World Bank power to change government policies and practices. Sociologist Goldman concludes about this practice: "Sixty years of this asymmetric triangular relation among the Bank, borrowers, and Northern firms has left borrowing countries highly in debt from their net capital transfer to the North. This bind gives the Bank a particular authority within borrowing countries, which it has mobilized to restructure a broad array of in-country institutions and social realms."[7]

In this chapter I will focus on the World Bank's role in the economization of education by tracing its original policies to its present role in global education. I will catalogue the different economic uses of education. It was during the McNamara years that the Bank expanded its education activities and initiated a worldwide effort to eliminate poverty. After the McNamara years, the Bank expanded its concepts of development resulting in a greater involvement in education policies. I will trace this evolution to its major report *The World Bank Education Strategy 2020*.[8] Again, I want to remind the reader that I am focusing on the World Bank's economization of education and, therefore, I will not be describing in detail its education projects, general complaints about its developmental policies and its internal operations.

From Reconstruction to Education for Development

Similar to OECD, the World Bank was established in 1944 to aid in post-war reconstruction. There are four distinct periods in the evolution of the Bank's policies. The first is simply loaning money for infrastructure projects, followed by the McNamara era from 1968 to 1980, and the Bank's dedication to end world poverty. During the third period in the 1980s the Bank fell under the sway of neoclassical economics (sometimes referred to as neoliberal economics) as discussed in Chapter 1. Since 1989, after protests about the environmental destruction by the Bank's projects, the Bank entered what has been called its "green neoliberal" period.[9]

In its early years, the Bank treated education as a tool for building an economic infrastructure in developing countries. Since its beginnings the World Bank has maintained a close relationship with the United Nations. Originally, the World Bank and the United Nations were to be part of a single system but in 1947 an agreement was reached making the World Bank a specialized agency of the United Nations. As a result, there are currently ties between the World Bank's education projects and the United Nation's Millennium Development Goals which include achieving universal primary education.[10]

The original articles creating the World Bank stressed its economic role and prohibited it from political interference: "The Bank and its officers shall not interfere in the political affairs of any member; nor shall they be influenced in their decisions by the political character of the member or members concerned. *Only economic considerations shall be relevant to their decisions* [author's emphasis]."[11] As the Bank leaders would discover it was impossible to disentangle political views from efforts to change so-called underdeveloped countries.

The Bank's original title, International Bank for Reconstruction and Development, indicates its original concern with the reconstruction of Europe.[i] While participating, in its early years, in European reconstruction, the Bank did focus on development issues as early as 1948 with a loan to Chile for agricultural machinery, and the following year with loans to Mexico and Brazil. As its work progressed from participation in European reconstruction to a primary concern with development, the Bank gave loans for infrastructure projects such as water supply, electricity, and transportation.[12]

These early infrastructure loans were not based on any theory of development. Edward Mason and Robert Asher write in *The World Bank Since Bretton Woods* that, to the question of "its failure to produce anything like a theory of development or even a systematic analysis of major permutations and combinations, it would no doubt reply that it is an operating institution concerned with lending and technical assistance."[13]

The goal was to encourage industrial development modeled on that of Europe and the United States. As sociologist Goldman writes, "In their view of development, modernization scholars start from the assumption that there is no alternative to Western-style capitalist development, that development unfolds naturally based on a set of laws of capital."[14] Providing an economic infrastructure was considered a necessary first step. But Bank leaders quickly discovered that providing capital resources was not enough since many developing countries lacked the ability to put them to use. Consequently, the Bank offered technical assistance, including education assistance, to aid in the use of capital for building infrastructures.

Introducing a new concept of education as an economic tool, World Bank planners treated education as a necessary condition for utilizing capital to achieve economic growth. Its Fourth Annual Report for 1948–1949 highlighted improving social conditions.

> Of fundamental importance is the low level of education and health prevailing in most underdeveloped countries . . . Without requiring any large expenditure of money, technical help in such matters as training teachers and doctors, establishing and operating schools for many different kinds, improving sanitary and public health facilities . . . can do *much, in the long run, as any other single factor towards creating the conditions necessary for accelerated economic progress* [author's emphasis].[15]

However, there was a tension between concerns about developing education and sanitary facilities and traditional banker concerns with repayment of loans.

---

i The World Bank Group currently consists of International Bank for Reconstruction and Development, International Development Association, International Finance Corporation, International Centre for the Settlement of Investment Disputes, and Multilateral Investment Guarantee Agency.

World Bank officials supported budget cuts and increased taxes to ensure countries could pay their loans.[16] The result in some cases was technical assistance to help education and demands for a reduction of government educational funding and cuts in other services. An example, which occurred in the 1980s as neoclassical economics became important in the Bank's work, were loans to Tanzania. Prior to the Bank's loans, Tanzania had primary school enrollments of almost 100 percent. As a condition for receiving a World Bank loan, the Tanzanian government in 1986 was forced to cut subsidies to public services. The result, as reported by education policy analyst Sangeet Kamat, was that "within a few years . . . enrolment rates [primary school] dropped sharply. Almost half of the country's children missed out on their legal right to primary school enrolment due to World Bank Reforms . . . the Tanzanian government could no longer subsidize primary education and had to charge tuition and other fees."[17]

In providing development loans, the World Bank contributed to the development of a world education culture. It is important to restate that the World Bank assumed that economic growth in developing countries would result in economic systems similar to non-Communist industrialized nations. At the time, the Soviet Union was offering an alternative economic system to that espoused by the World Bank. Also, most developing countries had Western-style education systems as a result of colonialism.[18] World Bank loans and technical assistance would continue to support schools similar to those found in American and European education systems.

Education Loans and Measuring Economic Growth

Until the 1960s, the World Bank measured development by the Gross National Product (GNP) and valued education assistance for its help in ensuring local populations could use the capital provided by loans. In the 1960s, Bank officials came to the realization that development would be a long process and that GNP was not an adequate measure of a country's economic health and the condition of its population. Bank officials also worried about income distribution. Increasing GNP might only benefit top income earners and leave behind an already impoverished population. Consequently, Bank leaders began to pay attention to the general welfare of the population, including levels of education. It slowly expanded its education loans to African countries, making its first education loan to Tunisia in 1962 followed in 1963 by the creation of an Educational Projects Division.[19] As a result, the World Bank became less of a bank and more of a development institution worried about more than giving loans. Political stability now became an issue when some developments failed because recipient nations were splintered by civil wars.

In the Bank's agenda, education became important for a variety of reasons beyond increasing GNP. Health, population growth, gender equality, and environmental conditions were now considered measures of a nation's welfare that could be aided by education. It was during the Bank presidency of Robert McNamara that these other factors became a focus of development discussions.

Putting Education to Work for Human Welfare: The McNamara Years: 1968–1981

Former president of the Ford Motor Company and US Secretary of Defense (1961–1968), Robert McNamara, in his first speech as Bank president, worried about the slow growth of income in Africa and South Asia where, he stated, "the peasant remains stuck in his immemorial poverty, living on the bare margin of subsistence."[20] Casting its shadow over this poverty was what he called "the mushrooming cloud of the population explosion."[21] Education would be considered a means of reducing population growth in developing nations.

McNamara presented a different perspective on the economization of education as he worried about the slowness of development projects. Education was enlisted to help reduce fertility rates by providing family planning information and by trying to get more women into school. While worrying about the elite Western-style schools introduced by the colonial powers, McNamara urged introducing new forms of education to circumvent the traditional education ladder. Consequently, under McNamara, the World Bank's plans made education an economic tool to increase GNP by providing administrators and workers who could utilize capital to build infrastructures, increase agricultural production, and combat population growth.

McNamara's first speech reviewed a new "development plan" proposed by the Pearson Commission; a commission recommended by his predecessor George Woods and named after its chair, the former Prime Minister of Canada Lester Pearson. Acting on the new development plan, McNamara recommended focusing on projects "which contribute most fundamentally to the development of the total national economy, seeking to break strangleholds on development."[22]

McNamara identified education as a priority, citing illiteracy rates of 30 percent in Latin America, 60 percent in Asia, and 80 percent in Africa. Adding personal fulfillment to human capital goals, McNamara asserted: "education is relevant to all aspects for development: it makes a more effective worker, a more creative manager, a better farmer, a more efficient administrator, a human being closer to self-fulfillment."[23] Unlike human capitalists in developed countries, developing areas like Africa were without the bare necessities for operating schools, particularly qualified teachers. This meant assistance for teacher training. And, he argued, these teachers must be supplied with the latest educational technology: "With the terrible and growing shortage of qualified teachers, all over the developing world we must find ways to make good teachers more productive. This will involve investment in textbooks, in audio-visual materials, and above all in the use of modern communications techniques."[24]

The Bank wanted educators to prepare local populations to efficiently use Bank loans. Development was not occurring as swiftly as once hoped for. Education was considered economically important to ensure projects funded by World Bank loans would be completed.

McNamara announced a threefold increase in education funding in his second report to the Board of Governors in 1969. The goal was more "trained human resources to use . . . capital efficiently."[25]

Similar to concerns expressed by OECD and the Chicago School of Economics about traditional education versus skills for employment in contributing to economic growth, McNamara complained that schools in developing countries, often modeled on schools of colonialists, were being preserved because of "traditional prestige."[26] He also questioned preparation for educational ladders leading from primary schools to colleges. This preparation, he argued, did not educate them "for the life they are likely to lead."[27]

McNamara wanted to ensure skills instruction appropriate to the needs of each country. Citing high dropout rates in African countries and unemployed educated workers in Asian countries, "The problem," McNamara told the Bank's Board of Governors, "is to sort out carefully the educational priorities from country to country, and to invest as selectively as possible."[28]

He summarized for the Board of Directors his position that schools should abandon traditional forms of education imposed by colonialists and focus on needed skills.

> In sum, in many countries of the developing world—countries entangled by a web of oppressive poverty which cannot be cut through until the *appropriate skills of the citizenry are honed and sharpened*—the educational complex is simply not relevant to the urgent needs of the society [author's emphasis].[29]

To ensure education met the economic needs of developing countries, McNamara laid out a World Bank agenda that provided technical assistance for "long-range education planning tied directly to the developmental strategy of the economy as a whole."[30] He argued that more attention should be given to functional literacy to remove, what he called, a major obstacle to development. Also, he called for the World Bank to provide less funding for school buildings and more technical assistance for curriculum development and preparation of teachers and school administrators. Citing the introduction of educational television in the Ivory Coast, he called on the Bank to finance educational innovation and experimentation. The following year, he could report to the 1970 meeting that the Bank had increased its education funding to reduce the "drag of functional literacy" on the economy.[31] At the same meeting, he announced that the Bank was beginning its work on population control.

Educational efforts to control population growth committed the Bank to changing family structures and, consequently, local cultures through family planning and the education of women. The Pearson Commission had warned that, "No other phenomenon casts a darker shadow over the prospects of international development than the staggering growth of population."[32] McNamara expressed his awareness that in dealing with population control the Bank was going to confront nations with their own particular social and cultural beliefs regarding the family and sexuality.

Consequently, education was considered a means to help economic development by changing social practices. "Educational systems," McNamara stressed at the 1973 Board of Governors' meeting, "should stress practical information in agriculture, nutrition, and family planning for both those within and outside of the formal school program."[33] He elaborated on the role of the Bank's education projects to limit population in a 1977 lecture at the Massachusetts Institute of Technology. The lecture asserted that there was no question "that expanding the educational opportunities of females correlates with lower fertility."[34] To support the contention that female education would reduce population growth he cited figures showing that in Rio de Janeiro, rural Chile, and Buenos Aires women having a primary school education had two children fewer than those without a primary school education. Also, something of cultural significance, women with primary school education delayed their age of marriage, thereby reducing their possible childbearing years. Education for both men and women, he asserted, increases their exposure to ideas of family planning and "enables them to learn about modern contraceptives and their use."[35] Also, parents with children attending school and not contributing to family income see them as having less economic value. Consequently, these families tend to limit their number of children. This pattern is reinforced, McNamara told the audience, in that when parents are educated they "typically desire an even better education for their children, and realize that if these aspirations are to be achieved, family size will have to be limited."[36] He concluded his argument with recognition of the role of education and family planning in changing cultures.

> Finally, perhaps the greatest benefit of education to both men and women in heavily traditional environments is that it broadens their view of the opportunities and potential of life, requires them to think more for themselves, and reduces their suspicion of social change. This creates an intellectual environment in which important questions such as family size and contraceptive practice can be discussed more openly.[37]

In the Massachusetts' lecture, McNamara stressed skills education in a manner similar to OECD. However, because he was dealing with the economics of development, the range of skills was much broader than those emphasized by OECD. In agreement with OECD, McNamara gave functional literacy and numeracy as important skills to be learned in school. But he added skills related to vocations, family planning, health, child care, nutrition, sanitation, and civic participation. Consequently, he asserted that to "create the demand for a change in family norm, governments should try to . . . expand basic education and substantially increase the proportion of girls in school."[38]

McNamara's last speech in 1980 to the Board of Governors contained a section on primary education that focused on the education of women. He now saw the education of women as a key factor in development. In other words, gender equality was made a function of economic goals. He asserted that:

> Women represent a seriously undervalued potential in the development process. And to prolong inequitable practices that relegate them exclusively to narrow traditional roles not only denies both them and society the benefits of that potential, but very seriously compounds the problem of reducing poverty.[39]

Citing the statistic that two-thirds of the world's illiterates are women, McNamara listed the economic benefits of female education. One was improvement in agricultural production since 50 percent of the work in farming in developing countries was done by women. He also stated educated women could find work outside of the home thus increasing their economic value to the family and general economy. And, as mentioned before, there were also economic benefits of reducing population growth by education reducing fertility rates.

McNamara believed that women's education was just as, or even more, important than the education of males because of the destructive nature of the population explosion. He stated, "In societies in which rapid population growth is draining away resources, expenditure on education training for boys is not matched by comparable expenditure for girls."[40]

In summary, McNamara broadened education's role in development to preparing developing populations to utilize Bank-financed capital to educating women. Human capital ideas slipped in when he argued for the necessity of education providing better human resources in the form of better workers, managers, and administrators. Education of women would ward off the economic drag of population explosion, improve agricultural productivity, and enhance the quality of the workforce. Similar to OECD, McNamara argued for a focus on skills instruction and new forms of education to break the hold of elitist education in developing countries. Also, he wanted a shift of funding from building schools to helping prepare more teachers and school administrators. And, similar to previous World Bank statements, McNamara assumed that the goal was to reshape traditional economic systems and cultures to look like those of existing industrialized countries. In this context, the World Bank's plans contributed to the development of a world culture based on the economic goals of multinational corporations.

The World Development Reports: Education as an Economic "Asset" in the War on Poverty

The World Bank declared education an economic "asset" as it tried to end the persistent poverty in developing nations. During the McNamara administration the World Bank began issuing World Development Reports describing its ongoing efforts to create a development plan that would end world poverty. The *World Development Report 1980* linked education and health services as important for economic growth. After a decade of experiencing a global recession and a debt crisis in many nations, the *World Development Report 1990: Poverty* proposed a development strategy that promoted free markets, investment in infrastructure and support of health and education.[41] The emphasis on markets in developing countries would affect the Bank's education strategy and included privatization of schools and finding new forms of education for developing countries.

Describing its anti-poverty efforts in the 1990s, the World Bank identified three strategies: "Promoting Opportunity," "Facilitating Empowerment," and "Enhancing Security." "Promoting Opportunity" included schools, development of infrastructure, and health services. The Bank described these efforts in the 1990s: "Overall economic growth is crucial for generating opportunity. So is the pattern or quality of growth. Market reforms can be central in expanding opportunities for poor people, but reforms need to reflect local institutional and structural conditions."[42]

Unlike human capital arguments that focused primarily on education as key to economic growth, such as in the United States, the World Bank emphasized "Facilitating empowerment" as necessary for ending poverty. Faced with corrupt and exploitive governments in many developing countries, Bank officials believed that organizing the poor was necessary to ensure that government services met their needs and that money loaned by the Bank was not lost to corruption: "The choice and implementation of public actions that are responsive to the needs of poor people depend on the interaction of political, social, and other institutional processes . . . Achieving access, responsibility and accountability is intrinsically political and requires active collaboration among poor people, the middle class, and other groups in society."[43] Of course, "Enhancing security," again something not focused on by human capitalists in countries like the United States, showed a realization that the poor were often kept poor as they were victimized by crime and war.

Therefore, the World Bank expanded the idea of poverty reduction from human capitalist ideas that were simply based on education and improving skills to cause economic growth that benefited all, to one that still included empowerment to ensure the poor benefited from government services and freedom from crime. Bank officials worried that income inequality in developing nations was hindering efforts to end poverty. Within this broader concept of poverty reduction, there was still a continuing effort to change developing nations from being primarily rural and relying on agriculture to urban-industrial societies.[44]

The *World Development Report 2000/2001: Attacking Poverty* provided a detailed plan for eliminating poverty in which education was considered an economic asset linked to other human assets. Influenced by the developmental economist Amartya Sen, the Bank added another dimension to the concept of development.[45] Sen argued that economic growth and income were not reliable determiners of a quality of human life. A better index, he argued was longevity which reflected the physical and emotional equalities of a person's life. A major contributor to longevity and quality of life, Sen asserted, was the ability of people to choose a life they wanted to lead.[46] Of course, the provision of health and education services contributed to these developmental goals.

Influenced by Sen, the 2000/2001 report provided a definition of poverty that required a variety of solutions. "To be poor," the report stated in a section on "The Nature and Evolution of Poverty,"

> is to be hungry, to lack shelter and clothing, to be sick and not cared for, to be illiterate and not schooled. But for poor people, living in poverty is more than this. Poor people are particularly vulnerable to adverse events outside their control. They are often *treated badly by the institutions of state and society and excluded from voice and power in those institutions* [author's emphasis].[47]

In addition, the report claimed to broaden the definition of poverty to include "vulnerability and exposure to risk—and voicelessness and powerlessness. All these forms of deprivation severely restrict what Amartya Sen calls the 'capabilities' that a person has, that is, the substantive freedoms he or she enjoys to lead the kind of life he or she values."[48] Reflecting Sen's argument, the 2000/2001 report states, "There is evidence that growth depends on education and *life expectance*, particularly at lower incomes [author's emphasis]."[49]

Education, in this broad definition of poverty, was considered an asset "synergistically" linked to poverty solutions. For instance, in Vietnam it was found that families with higher levels of education gained greater benefits from irrigation projects and in Morocco better rural schools resulted in greater use of health facilities. The report also highlighted the link between environmental conditions and the health of the poor. Thus education provides the poor with knowledge and skills to deal with environmental degradation and resulting health concerns. The 2000/2001 report stressed that, "Poor people are central in building their assets. Parents nurture, care for, socialize, teach skills to, and help finance the education of their children."[50]

The unequal distribution of public services was a major reason the World Bank called for empowerment of the poor. According to the Bank's calculations in developing countries the poorest 20 percent of the population received a smaller percentage than other income groups of public money for education and health. For instance in Kenya the poorest 20 percent of the population received 17 percent of the money spent on education and 14 percent spent on health services, while the highest percentage for both services was given to each of the top three quintiles.[51] The World Bank concludes, "public spending on education and health is not progressive but is frequently regressive."[52]

In calling for a redistribution of services, the Bank acknowledged its own lack of reliance on free markets in contrast to some human capitalist economists. First, the 2000/2001 report stated "markets do not work well for poor people."[53] Plus, the report stated, in contrast to economists who argued that simple economic growth would end poverty and inequalities, "public policy can reduce initial inequalities and increase the opportunities for poor people to benefit from growth."[54]

The Bank's call for empowerment is to result in arming the poor with the power to ensure equal access to public services, such as education and health. Even the poor should be globally organized. In his foreword to the 2000/2001 report, the Bank's president James Wolfensohn called for five key actions including, "Giving voice to poor countries and poor people in global forums, including through international links with organization of poor people." The Bank does rely on markets to empower the poor since provision of some of these services can include subsidization of purchases, such as vouchers for parents to choose an education for their children. In this context, choice becomes a method of empowerment. The 2000/2001 report calls for decentralization and greater community participation for school systems.

These proposals for ending poverty are strikingly different from those proposed for other countries, such as the United States. While twenty-first-century US education reforms to end poverty and inequality also include school choice, they did not include empowerment of the poor to participate in control of local schools and international education policies or equalizing spending. US policies rely on education to end poverty by ensuring everyone is taught the same standardized curriculum and school performance is monitored through testing. Also, US education policies lack the World Bank's holistic approach which includes concerns about health, the environment, and security. Nor have I found any suggestion from US school leaders that an important part of reducing poverty is to ensure that all people can live the life that they value.[55]

In summary, by the twenty-first century, World Bank officials expanded the idea of development from simply providing countries with capital for building infrastructure to a broader agenda of providing education and health services, empowering the poor, equalizing government services, ensuring the security of the poorest members of society, and helping people live the lives that they value. While there is a call for greater political participation, the issue of cultural differences seldom appears in the *World Development Reports*. The World Bank envisions an urban-industrial world that would be similar around the globe. In this context, education becomes an economic asset for achieving this urban-industrial world.

The Knowledge Bank: Economization of Knowledge

The best example of the economization of knowledge is the World Bank's statement that "Knowledge Sharing at the Bank is focused on: 'Putting knowledge on par with money'."[56] The World Bank's "Knowledge Bank" gives knowledge an economic value. In 1996, the World Bank launched the Knowledge Bank and in 1998 the Bank's World Development Report was devoted to the role of knowledge in development. The Report focused on two types of "how-to knowledge (farming, health or accounting) and knowledge about attributes (the quality of a product, credibility of a borrower, or the diligence of an employee)."[57] It added to development discussions the idea of a knowledge gap along with a gap in riches. The Report asserted: "problems with knowledge will persist, but by recognizing that knowledge is at the core of all our development effort, unexpected solutions to seemingly intractable problems will be discovered."[58]

Writing for the World Bank on Development Economics Through the Decades, Shahid Yusuf described how in the 1990s knowledge was "integrated into growth economics . . . knowledge offered a worthy alternative means of raising the growth rate."[59] This meant that the word "investment" could be associated with creating new knowledge (research) and its dissemination and impact. Also, the idea of a knowledge economy referred to economic growth being based on the creation of new knowledge to spur technological inventions. In this context, a knowledge bank creates and disseminates knowledge as part of a development strategy to enhance economic growth. For those who might wonder what happens to art and literature in this framework, the response would be that art and literature can be given an economic value.

This economization of knowledge is reflected in the 1996 World Bank statement under the title "Vision of a Knowledge Bank." Note the words "business," "value," "invest," and "clients" in the quote.

> We have been in the *business of researching and disseminating* the lessons of development for a long time. But the revolution in information technology increases the potential *value* of these efforts by vastly extending their reach. To capture this potential, we need to *invest* in the necessary systems, in Washington and worldwide, that will enhance our ability to gather development information and experience, and share it with our *clients* [author's emphasis].[60]

The World Bank's "Knowledge Bank" is organized to globally share knowledge to end poverty. The last of the three pillars of the Knowledge Bank is: "helping clients enhance their capacity to generate, access and use knowledge from all sources: Ultimately, the success of national development efforts depends on the trained human resources and institutional arrangements available to carry them out. Supporting countries to enhance their development capacity is therefore central to the Bank's mission of poverty reduction."[61]

The Knowledge Bank has even created an acronym that reflects a business model in dealing with research. It is EKMS which stands for Education Knowledge Management System. The Knowledge Bank, to illustrate its work, uses a diagram of the earth with arrows weaving in and out of it. One curving arrow carries the descriptor "Creating knowledge through learning from the outside world . . . research, evaluation." Another arrow is described as "Sharing knowledge with our partners . . . through products and services." The third arrow curving through the earth is "Applying knowledge."[62]

Knowledge usage, according to the World Bank, is essential to ending poverty. In its "Vision of a Knowledge Bank," it is asserted that "Lending alone cannot achieve poverty reduction."[63] Knowledge is treated as crucial, particularly the sharing of knowledge. Access to global knowledge is to complement local knowledge in the utilization of loans to fight poverty.

The economization of knowledge is reflected in the World Bank's education strategies. In its 1999 Education Sector Strategy it defined three factors affecting global economics. The first two factors, according to the Bank, are democratization and the development of market economies. The identification of market economies reflects the 1980s' infusion of neoclassical economics into the Bank's work. For market economies, the Bank asserted in its education strategy, which reflected the emphasis on skills discussed in Chapter 3, that: "Education is vital: those who can compete best (with literacy, numeracy, and more advanced skills) have an enormous advantage in this faster paced world economy over their less well prepared counterparts."[64] As mentioned previously, one form of knowledge championed by the Bank was knowledge about attributes which included knowledge about the quality of a product. This form of knowledge was considered crucial for a well-functioning market economy.

In the context of the 1999 report education becomes an asset in a market economy while knowledge becomes a driver of markets. In the description of the third factor affecting the global economy, knowledge becomes instrumental in promoting the other two factors, namely democracy and markets.

> Third, globalization of markets and the factors that drive them—especially knowledge—is reinforcing these impacts. Global capital, moveable overnight from one part of the globe to another, is constantly seeking more favorable opportunities, including well-trained, productive, and attractively priced labor forces in market friendly and politically stable business environments.[65]

Therefore, knowledge becomes economized in ensuring successful market economies and providing technical assistance to end poverty. This use of knowledge actually gives education a new economic function. In Chapter 3, I discussed the teaching of skills supposedly needed for global economic success. In the context of the Knowledge Bank, education provides the knowledge to succeed in the competition of products and people in the marketplace. Knowledge also makes it possible for global capital to find the right markets with good workers and a friendly government or, in other words, knowledge helps capital to receive a high return on investments.

The World Bank's Education Strategy

The World Bank's Education Strategy Review was issued in August 1995 two months after James Wolfensohn became the Bank's president. Wolfensohn not only initiated the Knowledge Bank during his term from June 1, 1995 to May 31, 2005, but also made education part of a holistic approach to ending world poverty. In a 1999 speech to the World Bank Groups' Board of Governors, Wolfensohn described his education initiatives to ensure the dissemination of knowledge to developing countries. This description highlights the World Bank's use of Internet technology to close the knowledge gap.

> Our Knowledge Bank brings us closer together through *distance learning* using satellite connectivity. And it takes knowledge to far-away places by closing the information infrastructure gap, reaching students through the *African Virtual University* and through our *WorldLinks* program connecting school children in the industrialized world with their brothers and sisters in the developing world.[66]

While the Bank's global education networks are important, I will be primarily looking at the Bank's economization of education which, under Wolfensohn, was tied to the economization of knowledge. The Bank's 1995 Education Strategy Review opened with a restatement of the human capital belief that: "Education is critical for economic growth and poverty reduction."[67] However, unlike OECD, the Bank gave more than an economic purpose to education. Writing the foreword to the strategy review, Armeane M. Choksi, Vice President of Human Capital Development and Operations, stressed education's importance for economic growth and ending poverty, but added: "Education is also about culture; it is the main instrument for disseminating the accomplishments of human civilization."[68]

While the 1995 Education Strategy Review repeated many of the claims of human capital economists, such as "Investment in education leads to the accumulation of human capital which is key to sustained economic growth and increasing income,"[69] it does present some new concepts regarding the economic role of education. First is the claim that education contributes to good government which is considered necessary for "sound economic and social policies."[70] What are these "sound" economic policies that will be supported by an educated citizenry? Reflecting the Bank's commitment to neoclassical economics, the answer is policies that promote free markets. The Review presents this equation for growth: "Education contributes to economic growth . . . The strongest growth comes about when investment in both human and physical capital takes place in economies with competitive markets for goods."[71]

Therefore, the Review emphasizes two important roles for education in free markets. One is providing consumers with the knowledge necessary to make choices in a free market. The second is to educate citizens who will support governments that have policies supporting free markets. The more cynical might say that these education goals are designed to propagandize for free markets over other possible economic systems.

Another new economic-education goal is helping workers adapt to job loss resulting from a swiftly changing economy. The assumption of the Report is that new technologies and economic growth in developing countries will cause workers to frequently change occupations. In the words of the Report: "These developments [technological change and sustained economic growth] have created two key priorities for education: it must meet economies' *growing demands for adaptable workers* who can readily acquire new skills, and it must support the *continued expansion of knowledge* [author's emphasis]."[72] These two education priorities are tied to the current idea that technological development is a driving force in global economic expansion. Education provides the knowledge to expand technology along with helping workers adapt to the economic changes it creates and their possible loss of jobs.

Two new economic-education goals were added to the World Bank's 1999 Education Sector Strategy. One was related to the movement of global capital and the other to sustainable development. Related to the movement of global capital was the previously mentioned role of education in market economies which, in this report, was presented as one of the "Drivers of Change." Claiming that 80 percent of the world's population worked in market economies, the 1999 Education Sector Strategy asserted: "Education is vital: those who can compete best (with literacy, numeracy, and more advanced skills) have an enormous advantage in this faster paced world economy over their less well prepared counterparts."[73]

Related to market economies was another "Driver of Change," namely globalization of markets including the global movement of capital. According to the 1999 Education Sector Strategy: "Global capital, moveable overnight from one part of the globe to another, is constantly seeking more favorable opportunities, including well-trained, productive, and attractively priced labor forces in market friendly and politically stable business environments."[74] According to the Bank, a role for education is helping workers adapt to this global movement of capital and the resulting changes in job requirements:

> Tomorrow's workers will need to be able to engage in lifelong education, learn new things quickly, perform more non-routine tasks and more complex problem solving, take more decisions, understand more about what

they are working on, require less supervision, assume more responsibility, and—as vital tools to those ends—have better reading, quantitative, reasoning, and expository skills. Again, education will be center stage: failure to recognize the importance of investing in human capital and equipping workers for the challenges ahead will handicap them severely.[75]

Education for sustainable development is part of the Comprehensive Development Framework supported by the 1999 Education Sector Strategy which is described as: "The Comprehensive Development Framework that the Bank is exploring rests on the conviction that social and structural issues are as important to poverty reduction and *sustainable development* as sound macroeconomic performance. Education, along with the rest of the human development agenda is getting greater prominence [author's emphasis]."[76] Sustainable development is an economic concept and therefore makes education for sustainable development another economic goal.

In the 1990s, sustainable development became part of the Bank's agenda after protests erupted about the environmental destruction caused by its many infrastructure projects, particularly dams. In the Bank's framework sustainable development economized the environment by giving it economic valuations, for example a money value to water, forests, and climate change.[77] When combined with a belief in markets, the World Bank's proposals often involved privatization, particularly privatization of water supplies.[78] In the Bank's economic language, the environment becomes "nature's capital."[79] In the framework of environmental economization, the Bank stated: "Earth's natural capital has been used in ways that are economically inefficient and wasteful, without sufficient reckoning of the true costs of resource depletion."[80] Consequently, education for sustainable development serves another economic function by helping students understand the cost of wasteful resource depletion and, consequently, the economic importance of protecting the environment. As part of the Comprehensive Development Framework, sustainable development becomes important in other policies linked to education, namely economic growth and ending poverty: "Sustainable development recognizes that growth must be both inclusive and environmentally sound to reduce poverty and build shared prosperity for today's population and to continue to meet the needs of future generations. It is efficient with resources and carefully planned to deliver both immediate and long-term benefits for people, planet, and prosperity."[81]

The 2005 Education Sector Strategy Update added "social cohesion" to human capital goals. The concern with social cohesion reflected a world in turmoil after the September 11, 2001 terrorist attacks on New York City's World Trade Center and the 2003 US invasion of Iraq. The 2005 Update contained a chart comparing it to the 1999 Education Sector Strategy. Added to the 2005 Update was "Education and post-conflict reconstruction."[82] With a world in turmoil, the 2005 Update declared it was "rooted in a vision of societies and economies that are increasingly dynamic, knowledge-driven, and cohesive . . . Realizing this vision requires education strategies that maximize the impact of education on economic growth and poverty reduction."[83]

Manpower planning, an original concern of the World Bank and OECD, appeared in the 2005 Strategy Update in discussions of workers adapting to ever-changing occupations resulting from free markets. It urged developing countries to "build a labor force that can adapt to shifting demands locally and in global markets" while "strengthening [its] education system responsiveness to labor market need."[84]

A striking feature of the 2005 Update was its continuing statement of beliefs that education could end poverty and cause economic growth despite the fact that poverty had not ended and economic growth seemed to be more affected by swings in the global economic pendulum than the availability of education. The importance of other factors to economic growth became apparent during the so-called Great Global Recession of 2008. The seeming failure of education to correct economic problems led to a questioning of the value of traditional education in contrast to an education focused on employment skills. The Bank's 2011 World Bank Group Education Strategy 2020 declared, "Given that global economic growth remains sluggish despite signs of recovery from the recent economic crisis, the shortage of the 'right' skills in the workforce has taken on a new urgency across the world."[85] As a result, the 2011 World Bank Group Education Strategy 2020, like OECD, focused on skills education as reflected in its title, *Learning for All: Investing in People's Knowledge and Skills to Promote Development*.

"Invest early. Invest smartly. Invest for all."[86] This phrase appears throughout Education Strategy 2020. The volume restated the World Bank's role in economic development and called for more preschool as an answer to poverty. The phrase is identified by Tamar Manuelyan Atinc, Vice President Human Development Network of the World Bank, as "The three pillars of our strategy."[87] The reliance on a skills agenda for economic growth and poverty is presented as: "The new strategy focuses on learning for a simple reason: growth, development, and poverty reduction depend on the knowledge and skills that people acquire, not the number of years that they sit in a classroom."[88] Discounting the importance of a school diploma, the Education Strategy 2020 declared, "At the individual level, while a diploma may open doors to employment, it is a worker's skills that determine his or her productivity and ability to adapt to new technologies and opportunities."[89]

Accepting the OECD claim that a two-hour test can predict a nation's future economic health, Education Strategy 2020 asserts that "recent research shows that the level of skills in a workforce—as measured by performance on international student assessments such as the Programme for International Student Assessment (PISA) and the Trends in International Mathematics and Science Study (TIMSS)—predicts economic growth rates far better than do average schooling levels."[90]

In Chapter 6, I will focus on the economization of early childhood education and the family. The World Bank's acceptance of the idea that early childhood education is key to ending poverty and advancing economic growth is captured in their phrase "Invest early. Invest smartly. Invest for all." Education Strategy 2020 declares: "First, foundational skills acquired early in childhood make possible a lifetime of learning; hence the traditional view of education as starting in primary school takes up the challenge too late."[91]

Conclusion: Loaning Money for Education to Grow the Economy, End Poverty, and Bring Developing Nations into the Global Economic System

I want to remind the reader that my focus is on the economization of education and that I have neglected many dimensions of the Bank's work. For instance, Education Strategy 2020 and the other Bank education strategies deal with a variety of topics including school management, financing, and teacher training. In addition, I have not elaborated on the many criticisms of the Bank's work. Some of the Bank's economic-education arguments echo the discussions in the last three chapters, such as education to end poverty, grow the economy, reduce inequality of wealth, and providing skills-based education. Therefore, I have concentrated on the Bank's unique contributions to the economization of education.

A unique feature of the World Bank's education goals is preparing the population to utilize capital and free markets. In the Bank's early years education was to provide the skills for utilizing capital generated by Bank loans for building national infrastructures. When neoclassic economics came to dominate Bank officials' thinking, education became important for dealing with the global movement of capital and preparing the population to participate in free markets. A perceived problem resulting from the global movement of capital and free markets was the constantly changing nature of the job market and global migration of workers.

The role of education in the global movement of capital and free markets was to provide lifelong learning to help workers adapt to constantly changing job requirements and the possibility of migration for better jobs. Education was considered necessary so that people would have the knowledge to make choices in free market economies. The Bank labeled education an "asset" in a market economy with knowledge being a driver of markets. In other words, education provides the knowledge to succeed in the competition of products and people.

Viewing the population explosion as a drag on developing economies, the Bank advocated using education to reduce fertility rates. Educational efforts to control population growth through family planning and the education of women committed the Bank to changing family structures and, consequently, local cultures. In the framework of the economization of education, the Bank supported policies to expand the educational opportunities of females because higher women's educational levels were correlated with lower fertility and, consequently, aided economic development. Also, it was believed that with education women could find work outside of the home, thus increasing their economic value to the family and general economy. Women's education was also to improve agricultural productivity in developing countries. Linked to women's education were proposals for early childhood education as part of the war on poverty. Early childhood education would supposedly free women to work and it would prepare children with skills wanted by global corporations.

World Bank officials argued for education to empower the poor to ensure that they received a fair share of government services. Facing corrupt and elitist governments in developing nations, political education of the poor was considered essential to the success of economic development. Also, empowerment of the poor was to result in greater security against crime which was considered necessary for economic development. Empowerment of the poor, at least in the thinking of the Bank's economist, would pressure governments to adopt positive economic policies, namely free markets. Education for political empowerment to ensure policies for economic growth is a unique characteristic of World Bank education proposals.

In creating the Knowledge Bank, the World Bank economized knowledge, or in their words, put knowledge on a par with money for aiding economic development. Also, knowledge was considered necessary for the functioning of free markets, to provide both knowledge to consumers so they could make rational choices in a free market, and knowledge for businesses to compete. Knowledge would also help in plans for sustainable development. Education in sustainable development was to help people think about the economic value of nature and the economic consequences of resource depletion and environmental destruction.

In summary, the World Bank expanded the notion of economization of education to include using capital; educating women; family planning; ability to operate in free markets; ability to adapt to changing occupational requirements; and empowerment to ensure equality of government services; security for the world's poor; and government policies favorable to free markets.

Notes

1 Michael Goldman, *Imperial Nature: The World Bank and Struggles for Social Justice in the Age of Globalization* (New Haven, CT: Yale University Press, 2005), p. xii.

2 Steven J. Klees, "World Bank and Education: Ideological Premises and Ideological Conclusions," in *The World Bank and Education: Critiques and Alternatives* edited by Steven J. Klees, Joel Samoff, and Nelly P. Stromquist (Boston, MA: Sense Publishers, 2012), p. 49.

3 Katherine Marshall, *The World Bank: From Reconstruction to Development to Equity* (New York: Routledge, 2008), p. 1.

4 Gita Steiner-Khamsi, "For All by All? The World Bank's Global Framework for Education" in *The World Bank and Education* ..., p. 11.

5 World Bank, "Economics of Education for Policymakers (Parts I and II) E-Learning: Objectives." Retrieved from http://web.worldbank.org/WBSITE/EXTERNAL/

WBI/WBIPROGRAMS/EDUCATIONLP/0,,contentMDK:21875447~menuPK:4 60937~pagePK:64156158~piPK:64152884~theSitePK:460909~isCURL:Y~isCURL: Y~isCURL:Y~isCURL:Y~isCURL:Y~isCURL:Y,00.html on September 18, 2014.

6 Michael Goldman, *Imperial Nature* . . . , pp. viii–ix.

7 Ibid., p. 155.

8 International Bank for Reconstruction and Development/World Bank, *Learning for All: Investing in People's Knowledge and Skills to Promote Development—World Bank Group Education Strategy 2020* (Washington, DC: International Bank for Reconstruction and Development/World Bank, 2011).

9 Michael Goldman, *Imperial Nature* . . . , p. 50.

10 Marshall, *The World Bank* . . . , p. 19.

11 Ibid., p. 27.

12 Ibid., p. 31.

13 Edward Mason and Robert Asher, *The World Bank Since Bretton Woods* (Washington, DC: The Brookings Institution, 1973), p. 468.

14 Michael Goldman, *Imperial Nature* . . . , p. 13.

15 As quoted in Mason and Asher, *The World Bank Since Bretton Woods* . . . , p. 461.

16 Ibid, pp. 464–465.

17 Sangeet Kamat, "The Poverty of Theory" in *The World Bank and Education* . . . , p. 35.

18 For development of Western-style education systems in European colonies see Joel Spring, *Pedagogies of Globalization: The Rise of the Education Security State* (Mahwah, NJ: Lawrence Erlbaum Associates, 2006).

19 Mason and Asher, *The World Bank Since Bretton Woods* . . . , p. 204.

20 Robert McNamara, "To the Board of Governors, Washington, D.C. September 30, 1968" in *The McNamara Years at the World Bank: Major Policy Addresses of Robert S. McNamara 1968–1981* edited by the Executive Directors, World Bank (Washington, DC: International Bank for Reconstruction and Development/World Bank, 1981), p. 4.

21 Ibid., p. 4.

22 Ibid., p. 7.

23 Ibid., p. 10.

24 Ibid., p. 10.

25 Robert McNamara, "To the Board of Governors, Washington, D.C. September 29, 1969" in *The McNamara Years at the World Bank* . . . , p. 75.

26 Ibid., p. 76.

27 Ibid., p. 76.

28 Ibid., p. 76.

29 Ibid., p. 77.

30 Ibid., p. 77.

31 Robert McNamara, "To the Board of Governors, Washington, D.C. September 21, 1970," in *The McNamara Years at the World Bank* . . . , p. 113.

32 Ibid., 122.

33 Robert McNamara, "To the Board of Governors, Washington, D.C. September 24, 1973" in *The McNamara Years at the World Bank* . . . , p. 255.

34 Robert McNamara, "To the Massachusetts Institute of Technology: An address on the Population Problem, Cambridge, Massachusetts, April 28, 1977" in *The McNamara Years at the World Bank* . . . , p. 407.

35 Ibid., p. 408.

36 Ibid., p. 408.

37 Ibid., p. 409.

38 Ibid., p. 431.

39 Robert McNamara, "To the Board of Governors, Washington, D.C. September 30, 1980" in *The McNamara Years at the World Bank* . . . , p. 639.

40 Ibid., p. 639.

41 World Bank, *World Development Report 2000/2001: Attacking Poverty* (Washington, DC: International Bank for Reconstruction and Development/World Bank, 2001), p. 6.

42 Ibid., p. 7.

43 Ibid., p. 7.

44 Shahid Yusuf, *Development Economics Through the Decades* (Washington, DC: The International Bank for Reconstruction and Development/The World Bank, 2009), pp. 19–21.

45 Ibid., pp. 34–35.

46 Amartya Sen, *Development as Freedom* (New York: Alfred A. Knopf, Inc., 1999).

47 World Bank, *World Development Report 2000/2001* . . . , p. 15.

48 Ibid., p. 15.

49 Ibid., p. 49.

50 Ibid., p. 78.

51 Ibid., pp. 80–81.

52 Ibid., p. 80.

53 Ibid., p. 79.

54 Ibid., p. 79.

55 For a general review of US school reform see: Joel Spring, *American Education 16th Edition* (New York: McGraw-Hill, 2014), pp. 193–271.

56 World Bank Institute, "Knowledge Bank: Overview." Retrieved from http://web. worldbank.org/WBSITE/EXTERNAL/WBI/0,,contentMDK:20212622~menuPK :575902~pagePK:209023~piPK:207535~theSitePK:213799~isCURL:Y,00.html on September 6, 2014.

57 World Bank, *World Development Report 1998/99: Knowledge for Development Abstract*, p. iii. Retrieved from https://openknowledge.worldbank.org/handle/10986/5981 on September 7, 2014.

58 Ibid., p. iv.

59 Shahid Yusuf, *Development Economics Through the Decades* . . . , p. 63.

60 Bruno Laporte, "Vision of a Knowledge Bank," PowerPoint slide in The Knowledge Bank in Action (October 8, 2004). Retrieved from http://siteresources.worldbank.org/ WBI/Resources/KnowledgeBankOct2004.pdf on September 5, 2014.

61 World Bank Institute, "Knowledge Bank: Vision." Retrieved from http://web.world-bank.org/WBSITE/EXTERNAL/WBI/0,,contentMDK:20212623~menuPK:575902~ pagePK:209023~piPK:207535~theSitePK:213799~isCURL:Y,00.html on September 6, 2014.

62 This diagram appears in World Bank Institute, "Knowledge Bank: Vision . . . " and Bruno Laporte, "Vision of a Knowledge Bank . . . ."

63 Bruno Laporte, "Vision of a Knowledge Bank . . . ," p. 9.

64 World Bank, *Education: Education Strategy Sector* (Washington: DC: The International Bank for Reconstruction, 1999), p. 1.

65 Ibid., p. 1.

66 James D. Wolfensohn, "Coalitions For Change," Address by James D. Wolfensohn, President of the World Bank Group, to the Board of Governors of the World Bank

Group (September 28, 1999), p. 10. Retrieved from http://www.imf.org/external/am/1999/speeches/pr02e.pdf on September 7, 2014.

67 The World Bank, *Priorities and Strategies for Education: A World Bank Review* (Washington, DC: The International Bank for Reconstruction and Development/The World Bank, 1995), p. 1.

68 Ibid., p. xi.

69 Ibid., p. 19.

70 Ibid., pp. 1–2.

71 Ibid., p. 19.

72 Ibid., p. 1.

73 World Bank, *Education: Education Strategy Sector* . . . , p. 1.

74 Ibid., p. 1.

75 Ibid., p. 1.

76 Ibid., p. 44.

77 Michael Goldman, *Imperial Nature* . . . , p. 10.

78 Ibid., pp. 221–270.

79 World Bank, "Sustainable Development Overview." Retrieved from http://www.worldbank.org/en/topic/sustainabledevelopment/overview#1 on September 8, 2014.

80 Ibid.

81 Ibid.

82 World Bank, *Education Sector Strategy Update: Achieving Education For All, Broadening our Perspective, Maximizing our Effectiveness* (Washington, DC: The International Bank for Reconstruction and Development/The World Bank, 2005), p. 20.

83 Ibid., p. 5.

84 Ibid., p. 9.

85 World Bank, *Learning for All* . . . , p. 11.

86 Ibid., p. v.

87 Ibid., p. v.

88 Ibid., p. 3.

89 Ibid., p. 3.

90 Ibid., p. 3.

91 Ibid., p. 4.

5

THE WORLD ECONOMIC FORUM

Partnerships and Entrepreneurship Education for Global Businesses

Founded to serve global business interests, the World Economic Forum's Global Education Initiative emphasizes human capital and entrepreneurship education promoted through partnerships between business, government, and civil society. Currently, the organization describes its membership, also explained in Chapter 3 regarding skill-based instruction, as: "Our Members comprise 1,000 of the world's top corporations, global enterprises usually with more than US$ 5 billion in turnover."[1] Meeting annually in Davos, Switzerland, the Forum networks leaders of major global corporations with politicians, leaders of nongovernment organizations, and other global and national people of importance.

The Forum has a significant impact on education as I learned in 2014 in my class on educational globalization when discussing the Forum's worldwide plans to integrate entrepreneurship education into all levels of education. A surprised student who taught young prisoners exclaimed: "We just received a notice this week of a training session in entrepreneurship education for teaching inmates." The same year, my institution, the City University of New York, was given funds by the state legislature for eight entrepreneurial programs.[2] Also in 2014, The Huffington Post reported that the Koch brothers were sponsoring entrepreneurial education for low-income high school students: "Youth Entrepreneurs, a nonprofit group created and funded primarily by Charles G. Koch, the billionaire chairman of Koch Industries. The official mission of Youth Entrepreneurs is to provide kids with 'business and entrepreneurial education and experiences that help them prosper and become contributing members of society'."[3]

Logically, as a business organization and private foundation, the World Economic Forum wants to pursue education policies that will benefit its member global corporations. With its slogan "Committed to Improve the State of the World," the Forum plays an important role in the corporatizing of global education by advocating partnerships between governments and business to manage national school systems. The organization brings together business, academic, and political leaders "to *shape global, regional and industry agendas* [author's emphasis]."[4] A goal of the World Economic Forum is to align the needs for global businesses with the goals of national school systems. The organization claims: "Companies are now actively engaged in dialogue with educational institutions."[5] It also recommends that: "Business should be involved in shaping curricula."[6]

The World Economic Forum grew out of the European Management Forum initiated by Klaus Schwab, professor of business policy at the University of Geneva, after a 1971 meeting of European business leaders in Davos, Switzerland. Setting the stage for future membership in the World Economic Forum, Schwab invited the top CEOs of European companies. After receiving an MBA at the Harvard Business School, Schwab called the meeting to help make European industries as efficient as those in the United States. Over the years, the interests of the European Management Forum went beyond management issues to general economic concerns of global corporations. In 1987, the organization changed its name to the World Economic Forum.[7]

The Forum's impact results from informal and formal conversations between global business leaders and others, and the Forum's published reports and initiatives, which serve as guides to how business can influence national government policies including education policies. Given its membership, it seems safe to assume that this influence over national policies is designed to help increase corporate profits. An important vehicle for this influence and a model for education planning is Klaus Schwab's multistakeholder theory of governance. This theory is the basis for partnerships between business and government in controlling education policies. As used in the Forum's first education initiative, the 2003 Jordan Education Initiative, the multistakeholder theory links national governments, global private sectors, national industries, academic experts, international and regional organizations, and local government organizations.

In this chapter, I will begin examining the influence the Forum's *Human Capital Report* has had on the economization of education and multistakeholder partnerships. This report ranks national economies according to the value of their human capital. In addition, the Forum launched education initiatives that support multistakeholder partnerships resulting in business partners influencing school policies. The chapter concludes with an analysis of its global entrepreneurship education initiative and how it is changing the curricula of primary, secondary, and higher education.

The Human Capital Report: Another Global Olympiad?

The World Economic Forum's Human Capital Index adds another Olympiad in world competition along with OECD's test scores. The World Economic Forum's *The Human Capital Report* ranks nations according to their "state of human capital development." The report joins the chorus of economists from

Gary Becker to those in OECD and the World Bank claiming education as a key to economic growth. It is laced with traditional comments about the value of human capital to economic growth. The preface was written by the Executive Chairman Klaus Schwab who opened the report with the assertion:

> The key for the future of any country and any institution lies in the talent, skills and capabilities of its people. With talent shortages projected to become more severe in much of the developed and developing world, it will be imperative to turn our attention to how these shortages can be met in the short term and prevented in the long term.[8]

The report's section on measuring human capital states: "In the business world, human capital is the economic value of an employee's set of skills. To the policy maker, human capital is the capacity of the population to drive economic growth."[9]

The evaluation of a country's human capital includes what the World Forum calls the four pillars of its index: Education, Health and Wellness, Workforce and Employment, and Enabling Environment. Indicators in the Education pillar are described as: "relating to quantitative and qualitative aspects of education across primary, secondary and tertiary levels and contains information on both the present workforce as well as the future workforce."[10] Health, which I discussed in Chapter 4 regarding the World Bank and the role of education in promoting health, is measured in the *Human Capital Report* by indicators of a nation's physical and mental well-being from childhood to adulthood.

The Workforce and Employment pillar is related to education through the use of indicators that include the skills of the population. The report describes these indicators as "designed to quantify the experience, talent, knowledge and training in a country's working-age population."[11] The Enabling Environment pillar measures a nation's support of human capital or, as described in the report, "the legal framework, infrastructure and other factors that enable returns on human capital."[12]

Exemplifying the economization of education are the global interlinkages between organizations in using international tests to measure human capital. The Education pillar of the Human Capital Index evaluates access to education, the quality of education, and educational attainment. Access to education is measured in enrollment rates for primary, secondary, and tertiary education along with education gender gaps. Quality is measured by

> PIRLS (Progress in International Reading Literacy Study); PISA (Program for International Student Assessment) math scores; PISA (Program for International Student Assessment) science scores; TIMSS (Trends in International Mathematics and Science Study) 4th grade math; TIMSS (Trends in International Mathematics and Science Study) 4th grade science; TIMSS (Trends in International Mathematics and Science Study) 8th grade math; and TIMSS (Trends in International Mathematics and Science Study) 8th grade science.[13]

Using all of the pillars, the World Economic Forum ranked 122 countries and found that European nations dominated the top ten having the highest quality of human capital.[14] The top ten in rank order were Switzerland, Finland, Singapore, the Netherlands, Sweden, Germany, Norway, the United Kingdom, Denmark, and Canada.[15] The only nation in this top ten that might be considered non-Western, though culturally it reflects its British colonial past, is Singapore. If these top ten in human capital quality are emulated by other countries then this could be another factor in creating a global world culture centered on Western values.

In the rankings, each pillar of the index is reported separately. Thus the rankings in the Education pillar reflect the qualities and test scores previously mentioned. The top ten in the Human Capital Index for the Education pillar in rank order are Finland, Canada, Singapore, Switzerland, New Zealand, Belgium, the Netherlands, Iceland, Ireland, and the United Kingdom.[16] Again this ranking favors Western and relatively small nations.

However, the results of the World Economic Forum's human capital rankings are quite different from results using only test scores. The reader is reminded of the statement in Chapter 2 that, "The gains in test scores over time are strongly related to [economic] gains over time."[17] And, as reported in Chapter 2, the top ten, combining PISA and TIMSS scores, in rank order are: Shanghai-China, Singapore, Hong Kong-China, Chinese Taipei, Korea, Macao-China, Japan, Liechtenstein, Switzerland, and the Netherlands.[18] Only two in this list, Switzerland and the Netherlands, appear in the top ten of the World Economic Forum's Human Capital Index.

The disparity in rankings between the Human Capital Index and test scores should be a caution for nations that rely only on test scores to judge their schools. For instance, in the Human Capital Index the United States ranks 16th in total quality of its human capital and 11th in the Education pillar. Using just the combined PISA and TIMSS scores the United States ranks 36th out of 65 countries.

While sample size varies between both rankings, the difference in rankings provides US and other countries' politicians and education leaders with a choice. They could criticize US schools for ranking 36th on PISA and TIMSS scores or they could praise US schools for being 11th in a combination of scores from PISA, TIMSS, and PIRLS along with measures of access to education; enrollment rates for primary, secondary, and tertiary education; and education gender gaps. Relying solely on test scores in discussing US schools ignores the US achievements in access to education, enrollment rates, and the education of women.

Multistakeholder Partnerships: Business and Schools

The World Economic Forum's promotion of multistakeholder partnerships helps global businesses in two ways. First, partnerships between government education services and business help to ensure that national schools are giving students skills wanted by global corporations. Second, greater educational investment in technology ensures a market for education products as I will describe later regarding Cisco's involvement in the Forum's Jordanian education initiative. Later, the World Economic Forum expanded its concept of partnerships to include "civil society and international organizations (UN bodies and multilateral donor agencies)."[19]

Schwab's multistakeholder theory is reflected in the organization's mission statement: "The World Economic Forum is an independent international organization committed to improving the state of the world by engaging business, political, academic and other leaders of society to shape global, regional and industry agendas."[20] A spokesperson for the World Economic Forum claims that the idea of partnerships emerged from the 1980s' rhetoric about free markets and the efficiencies of private companies. A partnership with business, including national education systems, would supposedly make schools more efficient in educating a workforce. The World Economic Forum's retrospective on partnerships asserts:

> The rise of neo-liberalism in the 1980s has had a lasting impact on subsequent partnership rhetoric through its emphasis on a low-tax economy and the efficiency of private enterprise. Driven by a belief that a shift from the public sector to the private sector will lead to efficiencies in government and thus greater economic well-being, the ideology emerged primarily in the richer countries of the world.[21]

Also influencing the World Economic Forum's partnership initiatives was the 1989 Washington Consensus. The World Economic Forum report on Global Education Initiatives claimed "The Washington Consensus argued for a shift in balance of activity away from the state towards the private sector, drawing into question the very meanings of 'public' and 'private'."[22]

For the purpose of defining the World Economic Forum's commitment to multistakeholder partnerships between business and national school systems, I am highlighting the Washington Consensus principle of "Privatization—state enterprises should be privatized."[23] It is important to note that this justifies for-profit schools. With this intellectual justification, the World Economic Forum launched the Global Education Initiative (GEI) with a partnership between Cisco and the Jordanian government. The Jordanian education initiative became a model for other World Economic Forum involvement in education.

The Forum didn't advocate complete privatization of schools since other sectors of society still valued government-funded public education as serving the public good. The Forum commented about the Jordanian education initiative, "Debate remains rife as to whether education should be delivered by the state or the private sector, or whether some kind of partnership between the two might provide the optimal solution."[24] As the debate unfolded it was agreed that partnerships should be multistakeholder partnerships (MSPs): "The diversity represented by the term MSPs is an important advance over the notion of public-private partnerships as it brings civil society and international organizations (UN bodies and multilateral donor agencies), alongside the state and private sector, in delivering effective development outcomes."[25]

Multistakeholder partnerships can link business interests with the work of the United Nations. These relationships clearly favor the interest of the global corporations belonging to the World Economic Forum. Within this framework, global corporate interests influence the educational work of national governments and their representative world organizations, such as the United Nations.

Multistakeholder partnerships are a compromise between full privatization of government services and the expansion of these services. One explanation for this compromise is that national government taxation of the public is a source of revenue for business. In other words, business can use the public purse to ensure that their agendas dominate school policies to educate a corporate workforce. In the same manner, technology corporations benefit from the use of public money allocated to schools to purchase their products.

Some technology companies are in the business of selling hardware and software to schools as documented in *The Great American Education-Industrial Complex: Ideology, Technology, and Profit.*[26] The importance of technology companies is reflected in the membership of the Steering Board of the GEI which includes major global corporations: Dirk Meyer, President and Chief Executive Officer, Advanced Micro Devices; John T. Chambers, Chairman and Chief Executive Officer, Cisco; Craig R. Barrett, Chairman of the Board, Intel Corporation; and Craig Mundie, Chief Research and Strategy Officer, Microsoft Corporation. The only non-technological member of the steering committee was from an investment firm: Lloyd C. Blankfein, Chairman and Chief Executive Officer, The Goldman Sachs Group Inc.[27]

In summary, multistakeholder partnerships open the door to business influence which can result in schools teaching employment skills wanted by multinational corporations. The partnerships are justified by a neoliberal doctrine of privatization that has been compromised by claims that education is a public good and therefore schools should be operated in cooperation with business. Thus, multistakeholder partnerships allow the corporate activities in schools to be funded by public revenues. In addition, technology companies can use these partnerships to ensure the use of their products in school systems.

Global Education Initiatives

The World Economic Forum launched its first education initiative in a multistakeholder partnership between Cisco, a leading technology company, and the Jordanian government. The Jordanian Education Initiative developed out of discussions at the 2003 Davos Annual Meeting. The discussion focused on how to use public-private partnerships to expand the role of information and communications technology (ICT) in primary and secondary schools. The mission statement for the Forum's GEI emphasized bringing the private sector into partnerships with national governments: "The GEI's primary objective is to raise awareness and support the implementation of relevant, sustainable and scalable national education sector plans on a global level through catalyzing *multistake-holder partnerships, in particular through the increased engagement of the private sector* [author's emphasis]."[28]

In the Jordanian Education Initiative, the technology giant Cisco teamed up with the Jordanian government to: "Improve the development and delivery of education through public-private partnerships and help the government of Jordan achieve its vision for education as a catalyst for social and economic development."[29] Besides seeing this partnership as contributing to economic development it was claimed that it would educate workers for building "the capacity of the local information technology industry for the development of innovative learning solutions in partnership with world-class firms, creating economic value that will lead to mutually beneficial business opportunities."[30]

At the initial meeting on GEI, according to a World Economic Forum document, "John Chambers, Chief Executive Officer of Cisco, along with many other CEOs present, proposed creating a collaborative partnership between business and government to transform education."[31] In their descriptive brochure of the project, The World Economic Forum cast the Jordanian initiative in the language of human capital: "Education is recognized as a key catalyst and enabler for social and economic development in countries throughout the world."[32]

The initiative fit Klaus Schwab's model for multistakeholder partnerships.[i] He believed that partnerships were the best means of influencing local governments. Writing the foreword to a report on the Forum's education initiatives, Schwab asserted: "The engagement of leaders from business, government, civil society and academia in action-oriented partnerships is *one crucial way the Forum shapes the global and regional agendas* [author's emphasis]."[33] Klaus then reiterated the human

---

i. There were many agencies and businesses partnering the Jordanian education initiative including: Aramex, British Council, CommercialWare/Corel, Computer Associates (CA), Cisco Learning Institute (CLI), Cisco Systems, Connectivity Partners International (CPI), Corning Cable Systems, Dell, DHL, Discovery Communications, e-dimension, Estarta Solutions, Fastlink, France Telecom, Global e-Schools and Communities Initiative (GeSCI), HP, IBM, Intaj (Information Technology Association—Jordan), Integrated Technology Group (ITG), Intel, JAID Productions, Jordan Telecom, Krach Family Foundation, Menhaj Technologies, Microsoft, Middle East Partnership Initiative (MEPI), MobileCom, NetCorps Jordan, Nortel Networks Kidz Online (NNKOL), North Virginia Technology Council (NVTC), Pearson, RAZORView, Reuters Digital Vision Foundation, Rubicon, Schools Online, Siemens, Skillsoft, STS, Sun Microsystems, Syntax, Talal Abu Ghazaleh and Company (TAGI), United States Agency for International Development (USAID), World Links and Young Entrepreneurs Association (YEA). See World Economic Forum, "Jordan Education Initiative a public-private partnership model for effective and advanced learning deployment" (Geneva: World Economic Forum and the Ministry of ICT of Jordan, 2004), p. 25.

capital argument in claiming partnerships between business and schools would help the world economy: "The challenges in education and the opportunities education provides as the enabler for economic growth and employment remain a critical global priority."[34] A Forum brochure on the Jordanian initiative assured readers that the multistakeholder partnership: "aims at enabling and accelerating social and economic development in the region and will result in a win–win for the private sector, government, local industry, and most importantly, Jordanian teachers and students."[35]

The Jordanian initiative linked the World Economic Forum to a project funded by the World Bank. Called Education Reform for Knowledge Economy, it was described as: "The largest ever education reform program presented to, appraised and approved by the World Bank."[36] Linkages between the World Bank and the Jordanian initiative helped to fulfill Cisco's desire to increase the use of educational technology. The purpose of the World Bank's project was described as: "To improve the quality of education for all students in the public education system . . . through . . . the deployment of new ways of learning through ICT."[37]

Profits for technology companies interested in cashing in on education seemed to prompt Cisco's involvement. Cisco and other ICT companies would economically benefit from widespread use of ICT in classrooms. In addition, Jordan had a stake in training more workers for the country's ICT industry and Cisco had a stake in finding technically trained workers and selling online instruction.

"By empowering our youth through this education initiative," Jordan's King Abdullah II Ibn Hussein wrote in the descriptive brochure about the Jordanian initiative, "Jordan and its World Economic Forum partners can create a dynamic and practical model of public-private partnership in the area of ICT that can ignite the engines of growth for future generations in Jordan and the region."[38] Claiming they were working for the "greater good" and not for profits, John Chambers, President and Chief Executive Officer, Cisco Systems Inc., hailed the partnership saying, "It is truly an honor to be part of such a groundbreaking educational model where private, public and non-profit organizations come together to drive the marriage of education and technology for the greater good."[39]

In the framework of the economization of education, Chambers linked education partnerships and technology to increasing the standard of living: "My hope is that the Jordan Education Initiative becomes the model for increasing the educational opportunities and standard of living on a global basis."[40]

A hope, which I am sure was supported by technology companies selling their wares to schools, was that the Jordanian initiative would be a model for developing countries. The link to the World Bank supported this goal. A stated purpose of the Jordanian initiative was to: "Encourage the development of an efficient public-private model for the acceleration of educational reforms in developing countries based on unleashing the innovation of teachers and students through the effective use of ICT."[41] Also a purpose was to create "an environment of national government commitment and corporate citizenship to build a model of reform that can be exported to and replicated in other countries."[42]

In other words, the World Bank's claims that education would cause economic growth supported the interests of technology companies represented by the World Economic Forum. The development plan emerging from the Jordanian initiative would make investments in education technology a supposed key to economic development. Following the pattern described in Chapter 4, this would mean that money from World Bank education loans would be used to purchase technology and software from companies based in developed nations, causing a cash flow from the Bank to the developing country to a global corporation.

The Jordanian initiative resulted in the opening of 100 "Discovery" schools.[43] There were other technology firms than Cisco involved in creating and managing Discovery schools. The initial study of infrastructure requirements brought together the Jordanian government, Microsoft, Hewlett-Packard along with Cisco. A Jordanian business supplied the schools with a learning management system called EduWave. Cisco provided wireless access, while fiber broadband connectivity involved a partnership with Corning Cable Systems and STS. The hardware/software for deploying the Math Online e-curriculum was provided by Cisco Systems, Dell, DHL, Hewlett-Packard, Intel, and Microsoft. IBM supplied the hardware/software for kindergarten schools. Intel and World Links, a World Bank project, implemented teacher training modules in Discovery schools.[44]

A popular business phrase "cash cow" can be used to describe the potential profits for technology companies in this education plan for developing countries. Imagine a steady stream of income from governments of developing nations to companies providing the education technology. Also, consider the possibility that this money comes from loans provided by the World Bank. While this circulation of money might provide educational benefits to developing countries it also provides profits to global technology corporations. Also, local businesses are supposed to benefit from these partnerships. In the case of the Jordanian initiative one of its claimed achievements was "the alignment of the needs and aspirations of the Government of Jordan, the local IT industry and multinational technology companies for the identification of potential business opportunities."[45] Local businesses work with the Information Technology Association of Jordan.

By 2009, the World Economic Forum had two other major GEIs with one in the Indian state of Rajasthan and one in Egypt. There were 26 multistakeholders in India and 37 in Egypt. Reflecting the business influence in these partnerships, the Confederation of Indian Industries is listed as the major partner in India. One goal of the Indian partnership was to advance the business agenda of selling more technology to schools: "The REI (Rajasthan Education Initiative) sought to bring a new educational paradigm to the state based on the following strategies . . . Deploy new technologies, particularly ICTs, for modernizing educational service delivery, skills development and quality learning."[46]

Educational technology was also highlighted in the Egyptian initiative and in another initiative for Palestine. The World Economic Forum education partnerships represented the business interests of its technology corporate members.

World Economic Forum Partnership with UNESCO

How do you economically profit from Article 26 of the Universal Declaration of Human Rights which states that "everyone has the right to education" and UNESCO's Education for All (EFA) launched in 1990?[47] For corporations represented by the World Economic Forum profits could be achieved by putting this human right and EFA into a multistakeholder partnership. EFA has six goals none of which were originally linked to privatization of education or the involvement of business concerns.[ii] Only the sixth goal touched on economic concerns by referring to "recognized and measurable learning outcomes are achieved by all, especially in literacy, numeracy and essential life skills."[48]

In July 2004, representatives of the World Economic Forum participated in a UNESCO-sponsored meeting on "Partnerships with the Private Sector in Education for All.[49] UNESCO's website asserts, "Public-Private Partnerships are expected to play an increasingly important role in the Education for All drive, creating an alternative source of funding for the Education for All goals and making more technical assistance available."[50] In 2005, the World Economic Forum joined a UNESCO seminar that "agreed on the need to build both global and local strategic alliances *between corporate, public and civil society sectors to enhance social and economic opportunities* for learners and to promote good practice in private-sector support to public institutions [author's emphasis]."[51]

Seeking help from the private sector, UNESCO worked with the World Economic Forum to create these partnerships. This was explicitly stated by UNESCO's Svein Osttveit, Chief, Strategic Planning and Monitoring, who explained, "Our partnership with the World Economic Forum was about the Partnership

---

ii. The six goals are: **Goal 1** Expanding and improving comprehensive early childhood care and education, especially for the most vulnerable and disadvantaged children; **Goal 2** Ensuring that by 2015 all children, particularly girls, children in difficult circumstances, and those belonging to ethnic minorities, have access to, and complete, free and compulsory primary education of good quality. **Goal 3** Ensuring that the learning needs of all young people and adults are met through equitable access to appropriate learning and life-skills programs. **Goal 4** Achieving a 50 per cent improvement in levels of adult literacy by 2015, especially for women, and equitable access to basic and continuing education for all adults. **Goal 5** Eliminating gender disparities in primary and secondary education by 2005, and achieving gender equality in education by 2015, with a focus on ensuring girls' full and equal access to and achievement in basic education of good quality. **Goal 6** Improving all aspects of the quality of education and ensuring excellence of all so that recognized and measurable learning outcomes are achieved by all, especially in literacy, numeracy and essential life skills. (UNESCO, "Education for All Goals." Retrieved from http://www.unesco.org/new/en/education/themes/leading-the-international-agenda/education-for-all/efa-goals/ on September 19, 2014.)

for Education . . . It was a direct continuation of the EFA movement, which was about partnership and broadening *this partnership by involving the private sector—we had not been particularly successful at this. Working with the Forum was a way to involve the private sector more* [author's emphasis]."[52]

In a 2006 publication, "UNESCO-Private Sector Partnerships: Making a Difference," UNESCO officials expressed their desire to work with the World Economic Forum to ensure partnerships with business. The publication explicitly stated that UNESCO partnered with World Economic Forum to create partnerships with major global corporations.

> In recent years UNESCO has worked very closely with the World Economic Forum—the Geneva-based foundation whose membership includes the world's 1,000 leading companies.
>
> *UNESCO shares the same view as the World Economic Forum that education is the key for sustainable social and economic development, and that there is a growing need to bring together global and local private sector companies to partner with governments* of developing countries to address the needs for the advancement of education in these countries [author's emphasis].[53]

UNESCO described a wide variety of partnerships with businesses and business groups.[iii]

UNESCO officials hoped that the relationship with businesses would be a source of financial support for EFA. Indeed, speaking for UNESCO, Dominique Morisse stated that the main reason for the partnerships was an expectation of "increased contribution from the private sector to education challenges through UNESCO education programmes."[54] However, she stated that this objective had not been achieved.

---

iii. ALLEVIATING BRAIN DRAIN IN SOUTH-EAST EUROPE a partnership with Hewlett-Packard; PROMOTION OF BASIC EDUCATION FOR MALAGASY CHILDREN a partnership with Rotary International, the Coca-Cola Company, and the French–Malagasy Chamber of Commerce; FIGHTING AIDS IN CHINA a partnership with the American Chamber of Commerce in China and Hoglund Foundation; MOBILIZATION AGAINST HIV/AIDS a partnership with the Global Business Coalition (GBC); REINFORCING MOBILIZATION AGAINST HIV/AIDS a partnership with the Global Business Coalition (GBC); "FOR WOMEN IN SCIENCE" a partnership with L'Oréal; PRESERVING INTANGIBLE CULTURAL HERITAGE a partnership with Samsung; GLOBAL ALLIANCE FOR CULTURAL DIVERSITY a partnership with 500 companies; and SAVING ENDANGERED LANGUAGES a partnership with Discovery Communications Inc.; SHARING BUSINESS SKILLS WITH CONSERVATION SITE MANAGERS a partnership with Shell Group; THE TOUR OPERATORS' INITIATIVE a partnership with the Tourism Industry; PROMOTING WORLD HERITAGE a partnership with the Media Industry. (UNESCO, "UNESCO-Private Sector Partnerships: Making a Difference" 2006. Retrieved from http://unesdoc.unesco.org/images/0014/001483/148376e.pdf on September 19, 2014.)

World Economic Forum: Business Partnerships and Entrepreneurial Skills

The World Economic Forum advocates teaching skills related to entrepreneurial education. The Forum's GEI Steering Committee signed a statement that: "We . . . believe that entrepreneurship results in increased innovation and sustained economic growth."[55] The Forum defined entrepreneurship: "Entrepreneurship refers to an individual's ability to turn ideas into action and is therefore a key competence for all, helping young people to be more creative and self-confident in whatever they undertake."[56]

A year after the great recession of 2008, the World Economic Forum released the report "Educating the Next Wave of Entrepreneurs: Unlocking entrepreneurial capabilities to meet the global challenges of the 21st Century" accompanied by the statement: "Entrepreneurship has never been more important than it is today in this time of financial crisis."[57] The report described entrepreneurship: "When we speak about entrepreneurship, we are defining it in the broadest terms and in all forms—entrepreneurial people in large companies, in the public sector, in academia and, of course, those who launch and grow new companies."[58]

Entrepreneurial skills are to stimulate the creation of new companies and to help corporate workers think "out of the box." As Klaus Schwab, Founder and Executive Chairman, reminds the reader in the previously mentioned report: "The motto of our organization is 'entrepreneurship in the global public interest', calling for entrepreneurs to put their ideas to the service of the global community."[59] Schwab claims: "Entrepreneurship and education are two such extraordinary opportunities that need to be leveraged and interconnected if we are to develop the human capital required for building the societies of the future."[60] It is also claimed that entrepreneurship education will help to alleviate the conditions of poverty by giving people the tools to create their own businesses.[61]

Representing some of the world's largest corporations, the World Economic Forum's Steering Board of the GEI gave a strong endorsement to their entrepreneurship initiative and offered another educational panacea to the world's economic problems in the form of entrepreneurship education.

> We . . . believe that entrepreneurship results in increased innovation and sustained economic growth . . . We believe entrepreneurial skills, attitudes and behaviors can be learned, and that exposure to entrepreneurship education throughout an individual's lifelong learning path, starting from youth and continuing through adulthood into higher education—as well as reaching out to those economically or socially excluded—is imperative.[62]

The report contends that multistakeholder partnerships will make possible the introduction of entrepreneurship education in national education systems.

The report's stated purpose was to influence "high-level policy-makers and leaders from the private and academic sectors who can work together to develop high-impact solutions through multistakeholder partnerships for embedding entrepreneurship education within their countries and regions."[63] The process was illustrated in the report's diagram "Entrepreneurial Ecosystem."[64] The diagram shows circular arrows leading from "Business: The Importance of Multistakeholder Partnerships" to "Government: Funding and Support" and from there to "Entrepreneurial Academic Institutions: The Changing Role of Academic Institutions" which include primary and secondary schools, higher education, and informal education. In the middle of these circular arrows and supposedly the beneficiaries of this multistakeholder partnerships are "Individuals & Intermediaries: Entrepreneurs, Champions, Foundations, NGOs and others."[65]

The plan to embed entrepreneurship education in national school systems demonstrates the potential effectiveness of multistakeholder partnerships. Business people, who might be influenced by the plans of the World Economic Forum, work with local government education officials to plan and implement entrepreneurial courses with claims that the courses will help the national economy. In addition, business people sit on university governing boards and can prod university officials to institute college courses in entrepreneurship. The multistakeholder partnership links business people to politicians who might be able to fund entrepreneurship education. This scenario is illustrated by the examples, given at the beginning of the chapter, of the New York State government legislating money for entrepreneurial courses in the City University of New York and the creation of high school entrepreneurial courses through the funding and influence of Charles G. Koch, the billionaire chairman of Koch Industries.

Reflecting this use of multistakeholder partnerships, the World Economic Forum recommends entrepreneurial education be a required course in colleges and universities. Combined with other skills instruction in academic institutions, entrepreneurial education is claimed to be a major contributor to economic growth. The GEI on entrepreneurship education recommends stakeholders to: "Encourage all faculties/disciplines to develop opportunities for students at every level to experience entrepreneurship. Integrate entrepreneurship into the curriculum and build towards a multidisciplinary learning environment."[66] The World Economic Forum recommends that academic institutions:

- Increase the number of schools offering entrepreneurship courses, programmes and activities
- Augment the number of entrepreneurship courses, programmes and activities and make them available to a broader group of students
- Make entrepreneurship a required course
- Integrate entrepreneurship across other disciplines
- Encourage entrepreneurship across disciplines, particularly in science and technology.[67]

Emphasizing the need for academic institutions to offer courses in entrepreneurship education, the European Roundtable on Entrepreneurship Education issued a "Manifesto" on entrepreneurship education declaring: "Governments across Europe must act now to address the growing skills gap."[68] Similar to the previously stated skills associated with entrepreneurship education, the Manifesto declares that educational institutions need to develop programs that provide the "appropriate learning environment for encouraging creativity, innovation and the ability to think 'out of the box' to solve problems." The Manifesto urges: "Academic institutions in Europe must revamp their programmes to enable the development of 21st century skills."[69]

Not just European universities, but also US schools, jumped on the entrepreneurship education bandwagon. In the previously mentioned New York State, funding of entrepreneurship courses in the City University of New York there resulted, among other programs, in the opening of the Goldman Sachs 10,000 Small Businesses Education Center at one of the university's community colleges to help "entrepreneurs grow their companies and create jobs."[70] The fact that the Center is located in a community college and not one of the senior colleges of the system indicates it, like high school courses promoted by the Koch brothers, is intended, in part, to help in the war against poverty. Second, the center is named after one of the companies represented on the steering committee of the World Forum's GEI by Chief Executive Officer Lloyd C. Blankfein of the Goldman Sachs Group Inc. The Center, as mentioned previously, is called the Goldman Sachs 10,000 Small Businesses Center.[71]

According to Christina Wilkie and Joy Resmovits, the Koch brothers' promotion of entrepreneurship in a high school with students from low-income families was "to provide kids with 'business and entrepreneurial education and experiences that help them prosper and become contributing members of society'" and to impart "Koch's radical free-market ideology to teenagers."[72] In the last school year, the class reached more than 1,000 students across Kansas and Missouri. Teachers for these courses are trained at Koch Industries headquarters where they are required to read Charles Koch's book *The Science of Success*. During the program's planning stage, Koch associates wrote, "We hope to develop students' appreciation of liberty by improving free-market education. Ultimately, we hope this will change the behavior of students who will apply these principles later on in life."[73] Reviewing the material and lesson plans for this program, Christina Wilkie and Joy Resmovits conclude, "Lesson plans and class materials obtained by The Huffington Post make the course's message clear: The minimum wage hurts workers and slows economic growth. Low taxes and less regulation allow people to prosper. Public assistance harms the poor. Government, in short, is the enemy of liberty."[74]

In other words, it can be argued that entrepreneurial education is a vehicle for spreading neoclassical economic ideas about the value of free markets. The general philosophy of entrepreneurship education assumes individuals are working in a free market to start and maintain businesses. It is assumed by advocates that an important route out of poverty is starting a small business. Consequently, entrepreneurship education targeting students from low-income families provides skills for business startups and inculcates a particular economic philosophy that doesn't threaten the functioning of global corporations. It becomes a back door to persuading students that attempts by governments to equalize incomes or expand social services will not help the poor but, in fact, will harm them. The message is that economic prosperity and income equalization will only result from entrepreneurs and businesses operating in a national economic system that has minimum government regulations, no unions, and free markets.

Entrepreneurship education has found its way into US colleges of education. For example, the University of Pennsylvania offers M.S. Ed. in Education Entrepreneurship which it describes as preparing students with skills to develop education businesses. Using the language of multistakeholder partnership, the program's website states it was: "Designed at the intersection of education, business, and entrepreneurship, the program combines Penn's rigorous academic study with practical coursework—giving you the tools necessary to chart entrepreneurial solutions in education."[75] Beginning in September 2014, *Education Week* began offering a series on what they called "edupreneurs." Opening the series, reporter Michelle R. Davis wrote, "Former educators with technology interests are increasingly making their way from classrooms into the startup world as they try to use their school expertise to create ed-tech products and services that solve common problems. What these new 'edupreneurs' are often lacking is the knowledge needed to launch and run a business."[76] Does learning to be an edupreneur also mean spreading the ideology of free markets?

So with the hope that entrepreneurship education will spark economic growth, save the poor, and propagandize for free markets, the World Economic Forum declared, "Entrepreneurship is a global phenomenon. The future, to an even greater degree than in the past, will be driven by innovation and entrepreneurship. It is time to more adequately develop entrepreneurial skills, attitudes and behaviors in our schools systems as well as outside formal schools systems, to reach across all ages as part of a lifelong learning process."[77] And, as suggested previously about the self-interest of technology corporations in education partnerships: "Throughout the report, the role of technology in delivering entrepreneurship education is evident, particularly in terms of creating greater access and scalability for entrepreneurship education."[78]

What effect is entrepreneurship education to have on a person's behavior? The hard and soft skills associated with entrepreneurship education include "creativity, new venture creation, business idea development and opportunity recognition, business planning, leadership, entrepreneurial marketing, entrepreneurial finance and growth management as well as soft skills like negotiation or presentation competences."[79] In reference to the Jordanian Education Initiative, H.M. Queen Rania of the Hashemite Kingdom of Jordan stated at a private 2007 meeting in Davos of the GEI, "Society faces a strong need to encourage people to 'practice at believing the unbelievable, using imagination, courage and tapping into the inner entrepreneur.'"[80]

Not surprisingly, the World Economic Forum admits that they do not have the means to effectively evaluate entrepreneurship education programs and, in fact, they do not have any proof that it in fact will accomplish its ends. The supposed outcomes from entrepreneurship education are a hope but not a reality. The previously cited report "Educating the Next Wave of Entrepreneurs" states clearly the lack of proof:

> While there have been many studies and research projects on entrepreneurship, to date, *there has not been enough empirical research on entrepreneurship education itself and its impact.* Longitudinal studies are not easy to design and implement, but they could provide better evidence of the impact of entrepreneurship education. Internationally comparable statistics and data collection is imperative as well [author's emphasis].[81]

That there was more hope than proof behind claims for entrepreneurship education is reflected in a statement on the same page as the above quote about lack of research by a member of the Steering Board of the GEI, Dirk Meyer, President and Chief Executive Officer of AMD: "Education is the clearest path to individual opportunity and societal growth, and entrepreneurship education is especially vital to fuelling a more robust global economy."[82]

Conclusion: Human Capital Index, Global Education Initiatives, Entrepreneurship, and Truthiness

From its beginnings under the leadership of Klaus Schwab, the World Economic Forum has used multistakeholder partnerships to fulfill many of its policy initiatives. On the surface linking business, government, nongovernment organizations, and civil society sounds democratic and promises policies that will be supported by the majority of the population. However, a multistakeholder partnership gives equal weight to the influence of business, civil society, and government. For the Forum's GEIs, this has resulted in major influence for business over national school policies. Business, of course, wants schools to educate workers in the hard and soft skills that they want.

With money and power, education businesses, particularly technology companies, are able through multistakeholder partnerships to exert greater influence over national school systems. The partnership of business, schools, and government has led to an increased purchase of education technology, profiting World Economic Forum members. The partnership with the World Bank has resulted in a scenario of the Bank loaning money to developing countries that, in turn, use the money to buy educational technology from global firms.

The World Economic Forum uses the rhetoric of human capital to justify its education initiatives. It also supports usage of international tests like PISA, TIMSS and PIRLS, by using them in their Human Capital Index. However, the education section of the Human Capital Index uses other indicators besides tests. The reader is reminded that some economists claim that test scores can predict the future quality of an economy. The Human Capital Index combines in its ratings test scores, access to education, enrollment rates, and the education of women.

Entrepreneurship was included in its motto and is now an important education initiative. Through the use of multistakeholder partnerships the push for entrepreneurship education in secondary schools and higher education is becoming a reality. As I discussed, entrepreneurship education becomes a back door for teaching the value of free markets. It is an ideology that stresses economic growth will result from giving entrepreneurs the opportunity in a free market to develop new businesses and ideas.

The ideology of free markets influences those advocating social entrepreneurship. For those opposed to government support of welfare programs, social entrepreneurship promises that social services will be provided by charitable or other private organizations and not the government. Boston College is a pioneer in offering degrees in social entrepreneurship through its graduate social work program. Social work education can emphasize government-provided services or a reliance on private organizations operating in a free market. The Boston College program supports entrepreneurship (innovation) in government and private agencies. Boston College's Graduate School of Social Work calls it: "A New Paradigm for Sustainable Social Change."[83] The program claims that, "Social innovation encourages the development of new ideas and directions for solving social problems, both creatively and effectively. Our aim is nothing less than transformative social change."[84]

Despite this somewhat left-leaning language about "transformative social change," the program's partnership suggests support of neoclassical economic ideas about competition and free markets. Following a similar partnership policy as the World Economic Forum in 2014 the Boston College program partnered with Ruta N Medellin in Medellin, Colombia to create an international Social Innovation Lab. This creates a partnership between Boston College and a corporation supporting technology businesses and competition in a free market. The website for the corporation describes Ruta N as: "a corporation created by the city of Medellin to promote the development of innovative technology-based businesses that increase the competitiveness of the city and the region."[85] The brochure for Ruta N highlights "Entrepreneurship Education: Science, Technology and Innovation."[86] The corporation stresses economic development through competitive free markets: "The current Development Plan 2012–2015 . . . [stresses]: 'Competitiveness for equitable economic development' . . . [and] focuses on Medellin's progress through the strengthening of its conditions of competitiveness and integration into the processes of globalization."[87] Therefore, even social entrepreneurship becomes a vehicle, similar to Charles Koch's high school entrepreneurship courses, to propagate support for neoclassical ideas about free markets.

'Truthiness' is a quality running through the literature of the World Economic Forum and other organizations and economists discussed in this book. Truthiness is a term coined by political comedian Stephen Colbert. It means stating as a fact something one wishes or believes to be true.[88] This is exemplified by the discussion in the last section about the World Economic Forum admitting that there is no long-term research proving the benefits of entrepreneurship education while, on the same page, a member of the Steering Board of the GEI claims entrepreneurship education will stimulate global economic growth. Is it possible that many human capital economists practice truthiness?

Notes

1 World Economic Forum, "Members." Retrieved from http://www.weforum.org/our-members on February 20, 2014.

2 "$55 Million Jump-Start for 2020 on 20 campuses: Gov. Cuomo Hails CUNY's 'Game-Changing' Entrepreneurship," *CUNYMatters* (Fall 2014), pp. 1, 6–7.

3 Christina Wilkie and Joy Resmovits, "Koch High: How the Koch Brothers are Buying their Way into the Minds of Public School Students," The Huffington Post (July 16, 2014). Retrieved from http://www.huffingtonpost.com/2014/07/16/koch-brothers-education_n_5587577.html on August 2, 2014.

4 World Economic Forum, "About Us: Our Mission." Retrieved from http://www.weforum.org/our-mission on February 16, 2014.

5 World Economic Forum, "Repository of Talent Mobility Good Practices." Retrieved from http://www.weforum.org/best-practices/talent-mobility/qualifications-adjusted-employers%E2%80%99-needs-project on February 16, 2014.

6 Ibid.

7 For a history of the organization see, Geoffrey Allen Pigman, *The World Economic Forum: A multi-stakeholder approach to global governance* (Abingdon, Oxon: Routledge, 2007), pp. 6–23 and The World Economic Forum, *A Partner in Shaping History: The First 40 Years 1971–2010* (Geneva: World Economic Forum, 2009).

8 World Economic Forum, *The Human Capital Report* (Geneva: World Economic Forum, 2013), p. v.

9 Ibid., p. 3.

10 Ibid., p. 4.

11 Ibid., p. 4.

12 Ibid., p. 4.

13 Ibid., p. 45.

14 Ibid., p. 11.

15 Ibid., p. 12.

16 Ibid., p. 12.

17 Eric A. Hanushek, Paul E. Peterson, and Ludger Woessman, *Endangering Prosperity: A Global View of the American School* (Washington, DC: Brookings Institution Press, 2013), p. 29.

18 OECD, *PISA 2012 Results in Focus: What 15-year-olds Know and What They Can Do With What They Know* (2014), p. 5. Retrieved from http://www.oecd.org/pisa/keyfindings/pisa-2012-results-overview.pdf on August 20, 2014.

19 World Economic Forum, *Global Education Initiative: Retrospective on Partnerships for Education Development 2003–2011* (2012), p. 8. Retrieved from https://openknowledge.worldbank.org/bitstream/handle/10986/5981/WDR%201998_99%20-%20English.pdf?sequence=1 on November 14, 2014.

20 World Economic Forum, "About Us: Our Mission." Retrieved from http://www.weforum.org/our-mission on February 20, 2014.

21 World Economic Forum, *Global Education Initiative* . . . , p. 4.

22 Ibid., p. 4.

23 See the World Health Organization's "Washington Consensus." Retrieved from http://www.who.int/trade/glossary/story094/en/ on February 18, 2014.

24 World Economic Forum, *Global Education Initiative* . . . , p. 6.

25 Ibid., p. 8.

26 Anthony G. Picciano and Joel Spring, *The Great American Education-Industrial Complex: Ideology, Technology, and Profit* (New York: Routledge, 2013).

27 World Economic Forum, "Educating the Next Wave of Entrepreneurs: Unlocking Entrepreneurial Capabilities to Meet the Global Challenges of the 21st Century" (Geneva: Global Education Initiative, 2009), p. 6.

28 World Economic Forum, *Global Education Initiative: Retrospective on Partnerships for Education Development 2003–2011* (Geneva: World Economic Forum, 2012), p. 23. Retrieved from http://www3.weforum.org/docs/WEF_GEI_PartnershipsEducationDevelopment_Report_2012.pdf on October 23, 2013.

29 Ibid., p. 13.

30 Ibid., p. 13.

31 Ibid., pp. 13, 23.

32 World Economic Forum, "Jordan Education Initiative a public-private partnership model for effective and advanced learning deployment" (Geneva: World Economic Forum and the Ministry of ICT of Jordan, 2004), p. 3. Retrieved from http://www.weforum.org/pdf/JEI/JEI-brochure.pdf on September 18, 2014.

33 World Economic Forum, *Global Education Initiative* . . . , p. 3.

34 Ibid., p. 3.

35 World Economic Forum, "Jordan Education Initiative a public-private partnership model . . . ," p. 3.

36 Ibid., p. 5.

37 Ibid., p. 5.

38 Ibid., p. 1.

39 Ibid., p. 1.

40 Ibid., p. 1.

41 Ibid., p. 7.

42 Ibid., p. 7.

43 World Economic Forum, *Global Education Initiative* . . . , p. 14.

44 World Economic Forum, "Jordan Education Initiative a public-private partnership model . . . ," p. 20.

45 Ibid., p. 24.

46 World Economic Forum, *Global Education Initiative* . . . , p. 16.

47 See Education for All, "Overview." Retrieved from http://www.un.org/en/globalissues/briefingpapers/efa/index.shtml on September 19, 2014.

48 UNESCO, "Education for All Goals." Retrieved from http://www.unesco.org/new/en/education/themes/leading-the-international-agenda/education-for-all/efa-goals/ on September 19, 2014.

49 World Economic Forum, *Global Education Initiative* . . . , p. 24.

50 UNESCO, "Education: Public-Private Partnerships." Retrieved from http://www.unesco.org/new/en/education/themes/leading-the-international-agenda/education-for-all/partners/public-private/ on September 19, 2014.

51 UNESCO, "Advancing the Education for All Initiative brings together the World Economic Forum and UNESCO." Retrieved from http://portal.unesco.org/en/ev.php-URL_ID=34333&URL_DO=DO_TOPIC&URL_SECTION=201.html on September 19, 2014.

52 World Economic Forum, *Global Education Initiative* . . . , p. 24.

53 UNESCO, "UNESCO-Private Sector Partnerships: Making a Difference" (2006), p. 5. Retrieved from http://unesdoc.unesco.org/images/0014/001483/148376e.pdf on September 19, 2014.

54 World Economic Forum, *Global Education Initiative* . . . , p. 25.

55 World Economic Forum, "Educating the Next Wave of Entrepreneurs: Unlocking entrepreneurial capabilities to meet the global challenges of the 21st Century (2009)," p. 6. Retrieved from http://www.weforum.org/reports/educating-next-wave-entrepreneurs on September 19, 2014.

56 Ibid., p. 9.

57 Ibid., p. 7.

58 Ibid., p. 7.

59 Ibid., p. 5.

60 Ibid., p. 5.

61 Ibid., p. 7.

62 Ibid., p. 6.

63 Ibid., p. 8.

64 Ibid., p. 10.

65 Ibid., p. 10.

66 Ibid., p. 28.

67 Ibid., p. 28.

68 Global Education Initiative, European Roundtable on Entrepreneurship Education, "Manifesto." Retrieved from http://www3.weforum.org/docs/WEF_GEI_European Roundtable_Manifesto_2010.pdf on February 24, 2014.

69 Ibid.

70 "$55 Million Jump-Start for 2020 on 20 campuses . . . ," p. 7.

71 Ibid., p. 7.

72 Wilkie and Resmovits, "Koch High . . . ."

73 Ibid.

74 Ibid.

75 University of Pennsylvania, Graduate School of Education, "M.S. Ed. in Education Entrepreneurship" Retrieved from http://www.gse.upenn.edu/tll/ee on September 20, 2014.

76 Michelle R. Davis, "Startup Founders Apply Education Experience," *Education Week* (September 16, 2014). Retrieved from http://www.edweek.org/ew/articles/2014/09/17/04startup.h34.html?tkn=LNXFlRvhH%2FKMIHdFPI12Rfjso5 9rtUjMqWQ9&print=1 on September 20, 2014.

77 World Economic Forum, "Educating the Next Wave of Entrepreneurs . . . ," p. 8.

78 Ibid., p. 11.

79 Ibid., p. 15.

80 Ibid., p. 9.

81 Ibid., p. 9.

82 Ibid., p. 9.

83 Boston College Graduate School of Social Work, "Center for Social Innovation." Retrieved from http://www.bc.edu/schools/gssw/csi.html on September 22, 2014.

84 Ibid.

85 Ruta N, "Home." Retrieved from http://rutanmedellin.org/ on September 22, 2014.

86 Ruta N, "Descriptive Brochure," p. 2. Retrieved from http://rutanmedellin.org/images/rutan/brochure_ingles.pdf September 22, 2014.

87 Ibid., p. 3.

88 Urban Dictionary, "Truthiness." Retrieved from http://www.urbandictionary.com/define.php?term=truthiness on September 22, 2014.

6

ECONOMIZATION OF THE FAMILY AND CHILDHOOD

Educating the Corporate Personality

As imagined in the novel *Fallen Land* discussed in Chapter 1, global corporations want family interactions to result in productive workers and children with the right soft and hard skills.[1] On the cover of OECD's *Human Capital* a nude baby is bent forward looking like he/she is either trying to stand or is at the starting line for the economic race.[2] In trying to educate the corporate personality, some economists and sociologists assert that the social capital of the family is key to providing children with soft skills to succeed in a corporatized global economy. I am using sociologist James Coleman's definition of social capital which refers to social relationships that help people to economically succeed or fail.

What happens if the family lacks the right social capital to ensure worker productivity and the children with the right soft skills? The answer of the economists discussed in this chapter is for children to attend preschool to compensate for the family's lack of the right social capital.

Is this a form of cultural imperialism? The World Bank, OECD, and the World Economic Forum propagandize for a family structure with the social capital that meets the needs of the corporate world without regard for other forms of family organizations and child rearing traditions. As I discuss in Chapter 4, the World Bank wants to change gender roles in developing countries to increase economic productivity and growth, resulting in changes in family organization.

In this chapter, I begin with an analysis of economic and sociological descriptions of the social capital of the ideal corporate family. Next I examine the global advocacy of early childhood education as a means of giving children the right social skills for economic success. This preschool section will focus on the work of Nobel Prize winning economist and member of the Chicago School of Economics, James Heckman. His analysis of a small sample of children in the longitudinal study of graduates from the Perry Preschool in Ypsilanti, Michigan is widely referenced in publications by the World Bank, the World Economic Forum, and OECD. While the Perry Study is used for the global promotion of preschool the limited numbers in the study and its cultural background in the African American community of Ypsilanti calls into question its global applicability.

Economization of the Family: James Coleman and Social Capital

A member of the University of Chicago faculty, sociologist James Coleman's work focuses mainly on US issues. However, like some economists in the Chicago tradition his work has entered the global dialogue about families and children. Coleman provides a framework for linking concepts of social capital with human capital and, consequently, relating the social capital of the family to economic productivity.[3] Coleman identifies two intellectual traditions with one, characteristic of sociologists, focusing on the social context affecting individual actions. The other, characteristic of economists, focuses on individuals acting independently in pursuit of their own self-interests. He argues that the two traditions can be brought together under the concept of social capital. Coleman describes how "social capital is productive."[4] One example is a market in Cairo where merchants help each other by taking a client who wants something not sold in their shop to another shop that does have the product. In this manner, the social relationships in the market are economically beneficial.

Coleman describes the distinctions between physical capital, human capital, and social capital: "If physical capital is wholly tangible, being embodied in observable material form, and human capital is less tangible, being embodied in the skills and knowledge acquired by the individual, social capital is less tangible yet, for it exists in the *relations* among people."[5] In this context, the family and school provide children with social capital that becomes part of their human capital which determines their future employability and economic success and their contribution to economic growth and productivity.

Regarding family factors influencing school achievement, Coleman divides them into three categories of financial capital, human capital, and social capital. Financial capital refers to family wealth and human capital refers to parents' education that contributes to a child's learning.

In the context of the corporatization of the family and its contribution to student achievement and economic growth and productivity, Coleman writes:

> The social capital of the family is the relations between children and parents (and, when families include other members, relationships with them as well). That is, if the human capital possessed by parents is not complemented by social capital embodied in family relations, it is irrelevant to the child's educational growth that the parent has a great deal, or a small amount, of human capital.[6]

Coleman provides an example of how family social capital contributes to the human capital of a child. Coleman explains that John Stuart Mill was taught Latin and Greek by his father James Mill and they engaged in critical discussions about his father's manuscripts. In this case the human capital of the father was transmitted to the son because of the social relations in the family which, in this case, is the interaction between father and son. In another example, an Asian family with low human capital, limited education, buys two copies of their child's textbook so that the mother can study it and help the child with school work. Therefore, the family's social capital (social relationships in the family) contributes to the child's education and human capital.

Therefore, from Coleman's perspective, strong relationships between parents and their children allow for access to the parents' human capital. He asserts, "The physical absence of adults may be described as a structural deficiency in family social capital."[7] Also, the lack of strong social relationships between children and parents, he argues, represents a deficiency in social capital. Coleman also claims that families with a large number of children may represent a lack of social capital because of the "dilution of adult attention to the child."[8] As I discuss later in the chapter, economist Gary Becker makes the same argument.

Using school dropout rates from his research of American high schools, Coleman identifies what he considers the ideal family structure for providing the social capital that will contribute to school success and the development of children's human capital. He controls for a family's financial and human capital in reaching these conclusions. The family structure with the highest social capital, he claims, is composed of: "two parents, one sibling, mother expects college."[9]

Other factors, Coleman claims, affect a child's learning. According to him, the number of times a family moves affects children because each move disrupts their social relationships and therefore diminishes their social capital. Also, Coleman finds the type of school children attend and their religious attendance influences their social capital. He uses school dropout rates to reach this conclusion. He claims that attendance at religious services is a measure of social capital. Public school students who do not attend religious services are more likely to drop out than those who do attend. Social capital is also related to the type of school a student attends. Using dropout rates as a measure of high and low social capital, and holding for differences in families' financial and human capital, Coleman concludes that religious schools (lowest dropout rate) provide the highest social capital, followed by secular private schools. Public schools had the highest dropout rate of the three types and therefore the lowest social capital.

Coleman also identifies other forms of social capital, such as close associations between parents and the school, which usually involve a mother's participation in school organizations and relationships with other mothers. However, this form of social capital declines, he argues, if the mother works full time. If the family moves frequently this social capital declines as association between parents and the school is disrupted.

In summary, Coleman's argument identifies family and peer relations that can contribute to a high social capital and will help to develop a child's human capital and the child's future contribution to economic growth and productivity. In this context, Coleman's ideal family's social capital that will contribute to economic growth and productivity is:

1. Two-parent household
2. One child
3. High expectations by mother for child to attend college
4. Child's attendance at religious services
5. Child attends a religious private school
6. Mother does not work outside the household
7. Family seldom moves.

Economization of the Family: Gary Becker

In 1981, Nobel Prize winner and University of Chicago economist Gary Becker published his ground breaking *A Treatise on the Family* which analyzed family life from the perspective of rational choice theory.[10] In Becker's words, reflecting the economization of the family, "In this book I develop an economic or rational choice approach to the family . . . an economic approach to the family, not in the sense of an emphasis on the material aspects of family life, but in the sense of a choice-theoretic framework for analyzing many aspects of family life."[11] The book was intended to provide, according to Becker, "a comprehensive analysis that is applicable, at least in part, to families in the past as well as the present, in primitive as well as modern societies, and in Eastern as well as Western cultures."[12] In other words, his intention was to present a global perspective on family life.

The book is based on free market economics and tries to demonstrate the negative effects of government intervention in the economics of the family. For this reason, free marketer Milton Friedman gave the book his endorsement: "This truly pathbreaking book marries techniques and problems hitherto regarded as utterly incompatible—rigorous economic reasoning to understanding the family . . . It is destined to affect the foundations of every science dealing with human behavior."[13]

Using rational choice theory, Becker, similar to Coleman, argues that government investment in a family's children discourages family investments. In the framework of rational choice theory, families make a rational choice about investing in their children. If the government offers money then, in this model, the family rationally chooses to reduce their investments. In discussing income inequalities between families, Becker argues that redistribution of wealth through progressive taxes and government spending for compensatory education will increase inequalities because if low-income families receive these government investments they will reduce their own attention to a child's needs.

It is important to note that no proof is given for the above argument. Also in the following quote on progressive redistribution of income to reduce income inequalities no proof is offered except for the unclear statement about "surprising implications of our analysis." Indeed, he suggests that redistribution will result in harming children in low-income families. Writing about a progressive system of income redistribution of wealth, Becker states, "One of the more *surprising impli- cations of our analysis* is that progressive taxes and expenditures may well widen the inequality in the long-run equilibrium distribution of disposable income, *essentially because parents are discouraged from investing in their children by lower after- tax rates of return* [author's emphasis]."[14] In the above quote I have underlined "implications" and "essentially because" as examples of hedging assertions with- out offering any proof.

Becker admits that family income influences the amount families can invest in their children. He introduces the concept of "luck" as a factor in these income differences. A child experiences "luck" in her/his "endowments" and in the "marketplace." Becker asserts: "The equilibrium income of children is determined by their *market and endowed luck*, the income and endowment of parents, and the two basic parameters—the degree of inheritability of *endow- ments and the propensity to invest in children* [author's emphasis]."[15] What are these family endowments that a child might be "lucky" to have inherited? For Becker it is a combination of family social capital and genetics: "Some children have an advantage because they are born into families with substantial ability, a strong emphasis on childhood learning, and other favorable cultural and genetic attributes."[16]

In other words, a child born into a low-income family might be "lucky" to have parents with the right social capital and genetics. These family conditions might result in low-income children succeeding in the competition for wealth in the marketplace. Of course, in the tradition of Horatio Alger's formula of suc- cess through "luck and pluck," luck in the marketplace affects economic success: "The income of children also depends on stochastic terms measuring their luck in the endowment 'lottery' and in the market for income."[17]

While endowments, social capital, and luck are important for children's future success so is family income. Family income and family size influence that amount families are willing to invest in their children: "expenditures on children are determined by the income and preferences of parents, the number of children, and the cost of child quality . . . Children from successful families are more likely to be successful themselves by virtue of the additional time spent on them and also the superior endowments of culture and genes."[18]

Similar to Coleman, rational choice theory predicts that family size will determine the amount of attention parents give to their children. Large families, Becker claims, reduce the amount of attention and investment parents can make in each child. A small family, ideally with one child, increases the amount of attention and investment. Becker could be accused of racism in the following quote on "quantity" of children and "quality"—families with substantial ability, who emphasize childhood learning, and have favorable cultural and genetic attributes.

> The interaction between quantity and quality also explains why education per child tends to be lower in families having more children, why rural fertility has approached and may even be less than fertility in advanced countries, and *why blacks in the United States have relatively many children and invested relatively little in each child* [author's emphasis].[19]

In economizing emotions, Becker recognizes that altruism plays a major role in a family's social capital. He uses rational choice theory to explain family altruism in contrast to what he calls the selfishness of the market. In this framework, people are altruistic in the family because it makes the family function better, while in the marketplace people are selfish for the same reason. In other words, people make a rational choice to be compassionate in the family but not in the marketplace. "I believe," Becker wrote, "that altruism is less common in market transactions and more common in families because altruism is less 'efficient' in the marketplace and more 'efficient' in families."[20] One might wonder if the world would be better if compassion and not selfishness played the major role in markets.

The reader is reminded that Becker is appraising the economic value of families around the world. If his reasoning is applied to world families it begins to sound like cultural imperialism similar to the World Bank, particularly regarding ideal family size. Based on his analysis, which recognizes the importance of luck in the family and marketplace, the economically efficient family has the right social capital, genetics, and a strong commitment to childhood learning.

What should happen if families don't have these characteristics, particularly the right social capital? The answer, as I explain in the next section, is preschool.

Heckman and the Economic Benefits of the Perry Preschool

Nobel Prize winning economist and member of the Chicago School of Economics, James Heckman, is the most active economist in defining the ideal character traits for economic success. His conclusions, as I will explain, are referenced by global organizations as proof of the value of preschool in curtailing poverty and growing the economy. The basis of his advocacy of preschool to eliminate poverty and increase economic productivity is a longitudinal study of graduates from the Perry Preschool. This study is cited by global organizations, as I explain later in the chapter, as proof of the economic value of preschool in teaching soft skills for economic success. However, there are issues about his interpretation of the Perry Preschool study regarding the sample size and applicability to other contexts, particularly other cultures and nations.

The Perry Preschool is often cited because it is one of the few longitudinal studies of preschool graduates. There are other preschool studies frequently cited, such as the Carolina Abecedarian Project and the Chicago Longitudinal Study.[21] However, Heckman and global organizations focus on the costs and benefits accruing to graduates of the Perry Preschool.

The Perry Preschool is located in Ypsilanti, Michigan and the longitudinal study tracks those who attended the school from 1962 through 1967 and examines the lifetime effects being reported by graduates.[22] The study includes 123 low-income African American children between ages 3 and 4 who were considered at high risk of school failure. 58 were in the Perry Preschool program while the other 65 received no preschool. The longitudinal study compared the effects of the preschool experience at ages 14, 15, 19, 27, and 40.

Important because of the global reach of the Perry Preschool Study is the sample size and location. How do the investigators that conducted the longitudinal study of Perry Preschool graduates answer the question: "Isn't the sample size too small to generate scientific confidence in the findings?" The answer seems to defy commonsense based on the researchers' conclusions about the benefit to all low-income students.

> Statistical significance testing takes sample size into account. To achieve statistical significance, group differences must become larger in magnitude as sample sizes become smaller. Indeed, a problem with very large samples is that educationally trivial group differences can achieve statistical significance. If the High/Scope Perry Preschool study sample were truly too small, none of its findings would have achieved statistical significance, and it would never have become influential.[23]

Despite Heckman and others frequently referring to Perry Preschool as proving the general economic value of preschool, the research group, High/Scope, suggests some limitations on its applicability to other situations. In answering the question about generalizability, High/Scope researchers state, "The external validity or generalizability of the study findings extends to those programs that are reasonably similar to the High/Scope Perry Preschool program."[24] By reasonable similarity they mean a preschool taught by certified early childhood teachers that serves low-income families, enrolls children 3 to 4 years old, and meets daily for 2½ hours.

In a global context, High/Scope researchers add a word of caution about its generalizability: "As the characteristics of a country's children and programs diverge from the characteristics of the Perry Preschool study's children and programs, applications become less certain."[25] While they argue the findings might apply to industrialized countries like Great Britain their generalizability to less industrialized countries "requires greater caution."[26]

Heckman has consistently cited the High/Scope Perry Preschool study without pointing out its small sample size and that for the findings to be generalized a school must have the same demographics and organization. In addition, he does not mention that the applicability of the study to other nations is limited.

Ignoring issues of sample size and limited generalizability, Heckman concludes his policy recommendations to foster human capital by claiming that lowering college costs is not as important as preschool: "Early investments in learning are effective. Much of the recent emphasis on lower tuition costs for college students is misplaced when the value of early preschool interventions is carefully examined."[27]

He also claims that significant improvement in the skill levels of American workers will not occur without early childhood education. For this reason, he argues that skill remediation programs for adults with educational disadvantages and training for displaced workers and older workers is a poor investment when compared to the economic returns from early childhood education. Using the same economic reasoning he does not believe that increasing subsidies, scholarships, and lowering college loan rates are wise investments. He argues:

> Students from low-income families tend to have much lower college attendance rates for reasons other than their inability to meet tuition and living expenses. Lower family income levels are associated with less productive family and neighborhood environments as well as lower motivation and ability by prospective students. These are factors not so easily remedied by student loans or fellowships.[28]

High/Scope,[29] the organization that conducted the Perry Preschool longitudinal study, found that those attending the Perry Preschool, at age 40, had a higher level of school completion (70 percent) than the control group (60 percent) who had no preschool. Other comparisons between those who attended and those who didn't favored preschool attendance:

1. A much larger percentage of program than no-program females graduated from high school (88 percent vs. 46 percent).
2. A smaller percentage of program females than no-program females had treatment for mental impairment (8 percent vs. 36 percent) and experienced grade repetition (21 percent vs. 41 percent).
3. The program group also significantly outperformed the no-program group on various intellectual and language tests from their preschool years up to age 7 on school achievement tests at ages 9, 10, and 14; and on literacy tests at ages 19 and 27.
4. At ages 15 and 19, the program group had significantly better attitudes toward school than the no-program group, and program-group parents had better attitudes toward their 15-year-old children's schooling than did no-program-group parents.[30]

The cost-benefit analysis showed more positive results for those who attended Perry Preschool than those who didn't. In the study, economic benefits were reported as education savings (less frequent attendance in special education classes and grade retention), taxes on increased earnings of preschool graduates, welfare savings, and crime savings (highest benefit).

The benefits from attending Perry Preschool were:

1. Savings from reduced education services, such as those resulting from grade retention or receiving special education was calculated as $7,303.
2. Taxes on earnings of Perry Preschool graduates were calculated as $14,078.
3. Welfare savings were calculated as $14,078.
4. Crime savings (arrests and incarceration) were calculated as $171,473.

The total public benefits are $195,621 with the cost for preschool attendance being $15,166.[31]

The study concluded, "that all young children living in low-income families should have access to preschool programs that have features that are reasonably similar to those of the High/Scope Perry Preschool program."[32] An implication of this study is that low-income families lack the human and social capital needed for success and, therefore, their children should have their social skills developed in an institutional setting.

Preschool, Soft Skills, and the Corporatization of Personality

In 2012, Heckman and his colleague Tim D. Kautz presented a paper on "Hard Evidence on Soft Skills" to the Annual Meeting of the European Association of Labour Economists which was later published by the National Bureau of Economic Research. In the paper, they claim "soft skills predict success in life, that they produce that success, and that programs that enhance soft skills have an important place in an effective portfolio of public policies."[33] They define soft skills as the "personality traits, goals, motivations, and preferences that are valued in the labor market, in school, and in many other domains."[34]

The authors assert that the personality traits associated with success in life are "conscientiousness, perseverance, sociability, and curiosity."[35] In the context of education these are the traits or soft skills families and schools should nurture to ensure individual and national economic success. They define conscientiousness as being organized, responsible, and hardworking and claim it "predicts educational attainment, health, and labor market outcomes as strongly as measures of cognitive ability."[36] Heckman and Kautz conclude: "Conscientiousness predicts educational attainment more than either of the facets of intelligence."[37]

Their essay contains a table that divides human personality into five personality factors including conscientiousness, openness to experience, extraversion, agreeableness, and neuroticism/emotional stability. The table shows the different facets of what they consider the character trait most likely to lead to economic success, namely conscientiousness. The following facets of conscientiousness describe what they think are the key traits for economic success.

1. Competence (efficient), Order (organized), Dutifulness (not careless), Achievement striving (ambitious), Self-discipline (not lazy), and Deliberation (not impulsive).
2. Related traits: Grit, Perseverance, Delay of gratification, Impulse control, Achievement striving, Ambition, and Work ethic.[38]

They also identify the childhood traits associated with conscientiousness and later economic success that could be used as a guide in trying to shape children's behaviors: "Attention/(lack of) distractibility, Effortful control, Impulse control/delay of gratification, Persistence."[39] Can the traits of conscientiousness be taught? Citing research, they state that 40 to 60 percent of character traits are inherited, leaving room for some development of character traits in the family, schools, and in later life experiences.

An earlier 2001 essay, "The Importance of Noncognitive Skills: Lessons from the GED Testing," coauthored by James Heckman and Yona Rubinstein and published in the *American Economic Review*, opens: "It is common knowledge outside of academic journals that motivation, tenacity, trustworthiness, and perseverance are important traits for success in life. Thomas Edison wrote that 'genius is 1 percent inspiration and 99 percent perspiration'."[40] This statement suggests that the identification of these soft skills for success might be based on the cultural values of the authors, particularly US cultural values and those of some other Western nations. This is highlighted by the sentence following Heckman's reference to Edison: "Most parents read the Aesop fable of the 'Tortoise and The Hare' to their young children at about the same time they read them the story of 'The Little Train That Could'."[41] No statistical evidence is provided that most parents read these books to their children. Also, since Heckman's work has a global influence, there is no evidence on how many parents in other cultures read these books to their children.

Heckman and Rubinstein's essay criticizes the reliance on cognitive ability in discussions of human capital. It argues that some people with high IQs are not economically successful because they lack the right soft skills. The essay compares high school dropouts, those passing the General Educational testing program (GED) and high school graduates on activities, such as skipping school in the last year, shoplifting, using illegal drugs, and being stopped by police to "demonstrate the quantitative importance of noncognitive skills in determining earnings and educational attainment."[42]

Their essay concludes that there is too much reliance on test scores to measure the development of human capital. They argue that: "A more comprehensive evaluation of educational systems would account for their effects on producing the noncognitive traits that are also *valued in the market* [author's emphasis]."[43] They go on to praise, similar to Coleman, the noncognitive values taught in Catholic schools.

A second conclusion stresses the ability to teach noncognitive skills as compared to raising IQ. They assert that IQ is set by the age of 8 and, therefore, schools after that age should emphasize the teaching of soft skills. Their policy recommendation is: "Given the evidence on the quantitative importance of noncognitive traits, social policy should be more active in attempting to alter them, especially for children from disadvantaged environments who receive poor discipline and encouragement at home."[44]

Using the language of economics, Heckman advocates greater investment in preschool education to develop soft skills. In his abstract to "Policies to Foster Human Capital," Heckman presents the simple formula: "Skill begets skill. Early investment promotes later investment. Noncognitive skills and motivation are important determinants of success and these can be improved more successfully and at later ages than basic cognitive skills."[45]

He calls education policies a "success" when the economic returns to society are greater than the public investment. Success for the individual refers to employment and income. A key to success, he argues, is education in noncognitive or soft skills. Heckman chides educational planners for relying too much on tests that measure cognitive skills as indicators of success. As noted earlier, he feels that cognitive skills must be complemented with the right soft skills to ensure success for the individual and economy.

For instance, he argues that education in soft skills would be the best investment strategy for aiding children from low-income homes to attend college. Introducing the social capital of families as a factor, he notes that children of high-income families attend higher quality primary and secondary schools. The social capital of higher income families, he asserts, provides the soft skills needed for academic success: "Children's tastes for education and their expectations about their life chances are shaped by those of their parents. Educated parents are better able to develop scholastic aptitude in their children by assisting and directing their studies. The influences of family factors that are present from birth through adolescence accumulate over many years to produce ability and college readiness."[46]

The central problem for low-income students, he argues, is not financial but family social capital and soft skills. Heckman feels that expansion of existing US loan programs and other subsidies will not be cost effective. There is enough money available, he feels, but the major issue is the lack of soft skills among low-income students: "Policy that improves the environments that shape ability may be a more effective avenue for increasing college enrollment in the long run."[47]

To increase college attendance of low-income students, Heckman concludes:

> If public policy aims to encourage college attendance, a focus on improving the environments of children and improving preparation for college will be

more effective than grant or loan programs to economically or cognitively disadvantaged children in their late teenage years. What is known about cognitive ability is that it is formed relatively early in life and becomes less malleable as children age. By age 14, basic academic seem to be fairly well set. Since scholastic ability promotes academic progress, early successful interventions in the life cycle of learning lead to higher overall achievement.[48]

In a similar manner, Heckman addresses the question of increasing educational attainment of low-income students in primary and secondary schools. Using a cost-benefit analysis, he asserts that "increasing spending per pupil is not a wise investment."[49] In fact, he suggests, the "U.S. may be spending too much on students."[50] His cost-benefit analysis found that increasing spending per pupil by 10 percent only yielded a 2 percent increase in future earnings.

Preschool for the World: The Cultural Imperialism of Success in the Corporation

The global diffusion of James Heckman's ideas about social capital and preschool has influenced policy statements by the World Economic Forum, the World Bank, and OECD. Consider the economic treatment of preschool in the World Economic Forum's publication *Education and Skills 2.0: New Targets and Innovative Approaches*. It claims: "Early childhood is being hailed by many economists as the smartest investment with respect to sustained returns in the form of individual learning and earning potential . . . and a way to narrow the gap between disadvantaged and advantaged young children and families."[51]

In advocating for preschool education, publications from the World Economic Forum, the World Bank, and OECD either cite each other's documents or James Heckman. In emphasizing preschool as a good investment, the World Economic Forum's *Education and Skills 2.0* references a World Bank project, *Investing in Young Children: An Early Childhood Development Guide for Policy Dialogue and Project Preparation*.[52] The following quote from the World Economic Forum's *Education and Skills 2.0* not only cites the World Bank publication, but it uses arguments similar to those of Heckman:

> On the cost side, investing in preprimary education has been linked to increasing the internal efficiency of primary school education by lowering its costs. Because children who attend preschool are less likely to repeat grades, drop out or require special education, significant cost reductions are realized in education budgets (Naudeau, Kataoka, Valerio et al., 2011). [This reference is to the World Bank's *Investing in Young Children*] Furthermore, there are decreased costs of public education, improved classroom climate and greater learning from peers (because some children are better behaved and children learn from each other).[53]

Both the World Economic Forum's *Education Skills 2.0* and the World Bank's *Investing in Young Children* use the same figure titled "Rate of Return to Human Development Investment across All Ages" with the source being Carneiro and Heckman (2003).[54] The figure shows the rate of return on investment for the early years of preschool to be close to 8 percent declining to a little above 4 percent at the age of six. From the age of six to 18 the rate of return declines to a little above 1 percent with a steady decline after 18.

The World Bank's *Investing in Young Children* also references Heckman in making the following claim:

> Remedial interventions are possible later in a child's development—such as education equivalency degree programs for school dropouts or therapeutic interventions for violent youth—but the longer a society waits to intervene in the life cycle of a disadvantaged child, the more costly it is to remediate the disadvantage (Heckman 2008a). Indeed, ECD [early childhood development] *interventions have not only a high cost-benefit ratio, but also a higher rate of return for each dollar invested than interventions directed at older children and adults* (Heckman 2008b; Heckman, Stixrud, and Urzua 2006) [author's emphasis].[55]

The Heckman articles cited in the above quote can be found in the following footnote.[i]

The World Bank's approach to early childhood education extends beyond economic and skills arguments to include concerns with emotional and physical health. Reflecting a growing world education culture and standardization, the World Bank uses the United Nations definition:

> The field of early childhood development (ECD) is framed by the United Nations Convention on the Rights of the Child, General Comment 7 (UN 2006) and refers to the physical, cognitive, linguistic, and socioemotional development of young children until they transition to primary school (typically around age 6 or 7). The first phase of human development (starting during pregnancy), ECD is an integrated concept that cuts across multiple sectors, including *health and nutrition, education, and social protection* [author's emphasis].[56]

It is important to note that this definition of early childhood education creates a global standardization of the term. It also explicitly includes in early childhood

---

i. J. J. Heckman, "The Case for Investing in Disadvantaged Young Children," in *Big Ideas for Children: Investing in Our Nation's Future*, edited by First Focus (Washington, DC: First Focus, 2008), pp. 49–58. J. J. Heckman, "Schools, Skills, and Synapses," Economic Inquiry, Vol. 46, No. 3 (2008), pp. 289–324. J. J. Heckman, J. Stixrud, and S. Urzua, "The Effects of Cognitive and Noncognitive Abilities on Labor Market Outcomes and Social Behavior," *Journal of Labor Economics*, Vol. 24, No. 3 (2006), pp. 411–482.

education, as noted in the above quote, "[t]he first phase of human development (starting during pregnancy)."[57] This standardized global definition of early childhood education from fetus to 6 or 7 seems to broaden Bruce Fuller's argument in *Standardized Childhood: The Political and Cultural Struggle over Early Education* about standardization of children in America to the global community.[58] Are the actions of the United Nations, the World Bank, OECD, and the World Economic Forum resulting in a globalized standardization of childhood?

Since the World Bank is loaning money and promoting its policies in developing countries its early childhood education proposals include concerns about health and security. However, these concerns are tied to economic goals: "Children who reach the end of early childhood should be developing well in the physical, cognitive, linguistic, and socio-emotional areas in order to fully benefit from further opportunities in the education and health sectors and to become *fully productive members of society* [author's emphasis]."[59]

In the context of the domination of English as the language of world business, the World Bank advocates as a goal teaching local languages in preschool, so that children are: "able to communicate in their native language with both peers and adults."[60] However, the emphasis on local languages in early childhood education and its assessments are, in part, designed to ensure that local populations are not alienated. The documents ask the question: "Are there any other constraints that prevent at least some families from using existing services?" The answer is that some parents might reject early childhood education for cultural and linguistic reasons: "as in the case of minority families who feel that existing services are not sensitive to their child-rearing beliefs and practices or their language or religion."[61] Therefore, recognition of local languages and religion is a tool to ensure participation of families in creating a global standardized childhood.

Of course, the economic arguments underlie the Bank's advocacy of early childhood education. The Bank's publication *Investing in Young Children* claims: "The skills developed in early childhood form the basis for future learning and labor market success."[62] It also emphasizes soft skills as an outcome of early childhood education: "ECD [early childhood education] enhances a child's ability to learn, work with others, be patient, and develop other skills that are the foundation for formal learning and social interaction in the school years and beyond."[63]

Despite its small sample size of 123 with only 58 actually attending the Perry Preschool and the caveat about the uncertain applicability to other nations, the World Bank cites the Perry Preschool Project as proving the economic value of preschool for developing countries. The World Bank does not mention the possible cultural differences between the African American population of Ypsilanti, Michigan in the Perry Preschool study and the loans it gives for education to nations in Africa, East Asia and Pacific, Europe and Central Asia, Latin America and the Caribbean, South Asia, the Middle East, and North Africa.[64] Are the culture and social conditions in places like India and Kenya the same as those in Ypsilanti, Michigan? The World Bank claims:

> A number of different ECD interventions . . . have been shown to positively affect school readiness and academic achievement. For example, participants in a high-quality, active-learning preschool program, High/Scope Perry Preschool, had higher rates of high school completion than the control group (71 percent vs. 54 percent), which in turn resulted in higher monthly earnings (29 percent vs. 7 percent earned US$2000 or more per month) and rate of home ownership at age 27 (36 percent vs. 13 percent) (Schweinhart et al. 2005).[65]

The reference to Schweinhart in the above quote is given as "Lifetime Effects: The High/Scope Perry Preschool Study through Age 40."[66]

Reflecting the global reach of Heckman's arguments, the World Bank lists four "Key Readings" for a chapter on "Invest in ECD? The Economic Argument" of which two are coauthored by James Heckman.[67] One of the coauthored Heckman articles is the "The Rate of Return to the High/Scope Perry Preschool Program."[68] Two other articles are about child development. In the reference section of the above mentioned chapter there are five articles coauthored by Heckman.[69] In the next section of the World Bank Publication, "Why Invest in ECD? The Survival and Health Arguments," there are four "Key Readings" with three being related to nutrition and the other to Heckman's "The Rate of Return to the High/Scope Perry Preschool Program."[70] In the next section, "Why Invest in ECD? The School Readiness and School Achievement Arguments," one of the four Key Readings is again "The Rate of Return to the High/Scope Perry Preschool Program," while the other three deal with nutrition.[71]

Heckman's work is also cited by Chinese scholars Xiaoyan Liang, Yu Fu, and Yinan Zhang in a World Bank-sponsored study *Challenges and Opportunities: Early Childhood Education in Yunnan*.[72] This study references Carneiro and Heckman (2003), *Human Capital Policy*, Institute for the Study of Labor (IZA) Discussion Paper No. 821[73] and claims:

> Attendance in ECD programs can also have a positive impact on individuals' educational attainment and productivity later in life . . . ECD proves to be a highly cost efficient educational investment . . . In the United States, the high-quality, active-learning preschool program High/Scope Perry Preschool also had a significant impact on . . . Those who enrolled in the program had higher rates of high school completion, higher monthly earnings, and higher rate of homeownership at age 27 than their counterparts who did not.[74]

The same figure on "Rate of Return to Human Development Investment across All Ages" that appeared in the World Bank publication appears in the OECD book, *Human Capital: How What You Know Shapes Your Life*.[75] Citing the previously discussed Heckman article "Policies to Foster Human Capital," the OECD book refers to the Perry Preschool study:

Nobel laureate James Heckman argues that investing in learning in early childhood brings higher returns than at any other time in life. There are social benefits, too. One US study showed that giving special support to under-fives from disadvantaged backgrounds reduced probation and criminal rates by up to 70% by the time the children reached their teens.[76]

Next to the figure "Rate of Return to Human Development Investment across All Ages," the OECD book reiterates Heckman's argument:

Nobel Laureate James Heckman argues that money spent on preschoolers brings returns that can't be matched at any other stage of life. Why? First, the earlier we're educated in life, the more time we have to earn returns on that investment. Second, learning young makes it easier to go on learning throughout life, which increases human capital and, thus, earnings.[77]

As the above discussion indicates, the economization of childhood and the family has become global. A standardized early childhood is embedded in calls for preschool education as James Heckman's study of a small group of students in an Ypsilanti Michigan is used globally to justify the economic outcomes of early childhood education.

Conclusion: Shaping the Global Corporate Family and Personality

Will a uniform ideal of family life and human personalities suited for global work be adopted universally? If this occurs many family traditions in different cultures would have to change to meet this ideal.

The ideal family, as described by the sociologists and economists reviewed in this chapter, is small with few children and has the social capital or internal social interactions that ensure a productive worker and children who have the soft skills to succeed in school and work. Coleman's list of ideal family characteristics includes one child and a stay-at-home mom who focuses on her children's education. He also stresses the importance of religious attendance and religious schools. Essentially, Coleman is economizing religion. In other words, he feels that religious values can contribute to the economic productivity of people. The problem with this argument is that many religions discount material goods for spiritual goods and hold compassion as an ideal in contrast to selfishness. If Coleman's ideal became a reality then religions would teach values and behaviors that help a person succeed in the marketplace.

Of course, Coleman's ideas might be parochial and just reflect the Protestant ethic dominant in American culture which stresses that the rich are rich because they are blessed by a god and the poor are poor because of weak character and that they can be redeemed if they change their character. The Protestant ethic was central to the McGuffey Readers which were the most popular school books in nineteenth-century America.[78] Coleman's ideal would require major changes in the world's religions to conform to his market-oriented ethics.

Using rational choice theory, Gary Becker arrives at a similar conclusion on family size. He uses the same concept of social capital as Coleman, only adding the argument that government education programs, particularly compensatory education programs for the poor, will result in the family reducing their investments and attention given to their children. For Becker the economically efficient family is small, has the right social capital and genetics and is committed to childhood learning. This argument contributes to a global ideal for family life.

James Heckman provides his ideal of a family's social capital to give children the right soft skills. If the family isn't doing this then, he argues, children should be sent to preschool. His list of personal characteristics will, he claims, lead to success in school and work. This list includes being organized, not careless, ambitious, not lazy, perseverance, delay of gratification, impulse control, and a good work ethic.

Missing from this list are behaviors like empathy, compassion, and altruism. As argued by Gary Becker, these emotions only come into play when they help social organizations to function efficiently. Becker argues that selfishness makes markets more efficient while altruism makes families more efficient. Thus emotions become a form of social capital that helps families and individuals become more economically productive. It could be argued that altruism in the marketplace could lead to a more socially just society. However, the economists considered in this book are focused on economic growth and worker productivity and not social justice. Therefore, at least in Becker's case, compassion has no positive function in the marketplace. Emotions are simply considered as utilitarian to the functioning of the economic system.

In summary, the corporate personality envisioned by these economists has the determination and grit to economically succeed with their emotions determined by their value in the workplace. Anger is not valuable in the workplace, but feelings of corporate loyalty would be. This economized personality shows all the characteristics needed for economic success but without the motivation to struggle for political and social justice. Their households are organized by the social capital needed for breadwinners to succeed and children prepared to learn how to be good workers.

Notes

1 Patrick Flanery, *Fallen Land* (New York: Riverhead Books, 2013).
2 Brian Keeley, *Human Capital: How What You Know Shapes Your Life* (Paris: OECD Publishing, 2007).
3 James S. Coleman, "Social Capital in the Creation of Human Capital," *The American Journal of Sociology*, Vol. 94 (1988), pp. 95–120.
4 Ibid., p. 98.
5 Ibid., pp. 100–101.

6 Ibid., p. 110.

7 Ibid., p. 111.

8 Ibid., p. 111.

9 Ibid., p. 112.

10 Gary S. Becker, *A Treatise on the Family: Enlarged Edition* (Cambridge: Harvard University Press, 1991).

11 Ibid., p. ix.

12 Ibid., p. 10.

13 Ibid., Milton Friedman backcover endorsement.

14 Ibid., p. 231.

15 Ibid., p. 230.

16 Ibid., p. 241.

17 Ibid., p. 230.

18 Ibid., p. 179.

19 Ibid., p. 135.

20 Ibid., p. 299.

21 See Frances A. Campbell et al., "Adult Outcomes as a Function of an Early Childhood Educational Program: An Abecedarian Project Follow-Up," *Developmental Psychology* (2012), Vol. 48, No. 4, 1033–1043 and Waisman Center, *Chicago Longitudinal Study* Issue 1, August 2000, retrieved from http://www.waisman.wisc.edu/cls/NEWSLETN.PDF on November 21, 2013.

22 Lawrence J. Schweinhart et al., "The High/Scope Perry Preschool Study Through Age 40: Summary, Conclusions, and Frequently Asked Questions," (Ypsilanti Michigan, High/Scope Press, 2005). Retrieved from http://www.highscope.org/file/Research/PerryProject/specialsummary_rev2011_02_2.pdf on November 13, 2013.

23 Schweinhart et al., "The High/Scope Perry Preschool Study . . . ," p. 7.

24 Ibid., pp. 7–8.

25 Ibid., p. 11.

26 Ibid., p. 13.

27 Ibid., p. 42.

28 Ibid., p. 43.

29 See High/Scope, "About Us." Retrieved from http://www.highscope.org/Content.asp?ContentId=761 on March 17, 2014.

30 Schweinhart et al., "The High/Scope Perry Preschool Study . . . , p. 1.

31 Ibid., pp. 3–4.

32 Ibid., p. 5.

33 James Heckman and Tim D. Kautz, "Hard Evidence on Soft Skills" (Cambridge, MA: National Bureau of Economic Research, 2012), p. 2.

34 Ibid., p. 2.

35 Ibid., p. 3.

36 Ibid., p. 5.

37 Ibid., p. 18.

38 Ibid., p.13.

39 Ibid., p. 13.

40 James J. Heckman and Yona Rubinstein, "The Importance of Noncognitive Skills: Lessons from the GED Testing Program," *The American Economic Review*, Vol. 91, No. 2 (May, 2001), p. 145.

41 Ibid., p. 145.

42 Ibid., p. 146.

43 Ibid., p. 148.

44 Ibid., pp. 148–149.

45 James J. Heckman, "Policies to Foster Human Capital," National Bureau of Economic Research (August, 1999), p. i. Retrieved from http://www.nber.org/papers/w7288 on February 10, 2014.

46 Ibid., p. 13.

47 Ibid., p. 13.

48 Ibid., p. 14.

49 Ibid., p. 18.

50 Ibid., p. 19.

51 World Economic Forum, *Education and Skills 2.0: New Targets and Innovative Approaches* (Geneva: World Economic Forum, January 2014), p. 18.

52 Sophie Naudeau, Naoko Kataoka, Alexandria Valerio, Michelle J. Neuman, and Leslie Kennedy Elder, *Investing in Young Children: An Early Childhood Development Guide for Policy Dialogue and Project Preparation*, (Washington, DC: World Bank, 2011) and World Economic Forum, *Education and Skills 2.0 . . . .*

53 World Economic Forum, *Education and Skills 2.0 . . .* , p. 18.

54 Naudeau et al., *Investing in Young Children . . .* , p. 19. The reference is cited by Naudeau as P. Carneiro and J. Heckman, "Human Capital Policy." NBER Working Paper 9495 (Cambridge, MA: National Bureau of Economic Research, 2003).

55 Ibid., p. 19.

56 Ibid., p. 5.

57 Ibid., p. 5.

58 Bruce Fuller, *Standardized Childhood: The Political and Cultural Struggle over Early Education* (Palo Alto: Stanford University Press, 2008).

59 Naudeau et al., *Investing in Young Children . . .* , p. 5.

60 Ibid., p. 5.

61 Ibid., p. 53.

62 Ibid., p. 15.

63 Ibid., p. 15.

64 The World Bank, "Countries." Retrieved from http://www.worldbank.org/en/country on March 12, 2014.

65 Ibid., p. 18.

66 Ibid., p. 23. Regarding the Schweinhart reference in the World Bank publication see the previous endnote. Lawrence J. Schweinhart et al., "The High/Scope Perry Preschool Study . . . ."

67 Naudeau et al., *Investing in Young Children . . .* , "Why Invest in ECD? The Economic Argument," p. 21. The key readings include, Heckman, J. J., and D. V. Masterov, "The Productivity Argument for Investing in Young Children." *Review of Agricultural Economics*, Vol. 29, No. 3(2007), pp. 446–93; Heckman, J. J., S. H. Moon, R. Pinto, P. A. Savalyev, and A. Yavitz, "The Rate of Return to the High/Scope Perry Preschool Program." Working Paper 200936 (Geary Institute, University College Dublin, 2009). http://www.ucd.ie/geary/static/publications/workingpapers/gearywp200936.pdf.

68 Ibid.

69 Ibid., p. 22. The five articles are: J. J. Heckman, "The Case for Investing in Disadvantaged Young Children," in *Big Ideas for Children: Investing in Our Nation's Future*, edited by First Focus (Washington, DC: First Focus, 2008), pp. 49–58; J. J. Heckman, "Schools, Skills, and Synapses," Economic Inquiry, Vol. 46, No. 3 (2008), pp. 289–324; J. J. Heckman and

D.V. Masterov, "The Productivity Argument for Investing in Young Children," *Review of Agricultural Economics*, Vol. 29, No. 3 (2007), pp. 446–493; J. J. Heckman et al., "The Rate of Return to the High/Scope Perry Preschool Program . . . "; J. J. Heckman, J. Stixrud, and S. Urzua, "The Effects of Cognitive and Noncognitive Abilities on Labor Market Outcomes and Social Behavior," *Journal of Labor Economics*, Vol. 24, No. 3 (2006), pp. 411–482.

70 Naudeau et al., *Investing in Young Children* . . . , "Why Invest in ECD? The Survival and Health Arguments," p. 32.

71 Naudeau et al., *Investing in Young Children* . . . , "Why Invest in ECD? The School Readiness and School Achievement Arguments," p. 32.

72 Xiaoyan Liang, Yu Fu, and Yinan Zhang, *Challenges and Opportunities: Early Childhood Education in Yunnan* (World Bank Document, November 18, 2013). Retrieved from http://documents.worldbank.org/curated/en/2013/11/20116721/china-early-child-development-early-childhood-education-yunnan on October 5, 2014.

73 Ibid., p. 40.

74 Ibid., p. 39.

75 Brian Keeley, *Human Capital* (Paris: OECD, 2007).

76 Ibid., p. 42.

77 Ibid., p. 42.

78 See Joel Spring, *The American School A Global Context: From the Puritans to the Obama Administration* Ninth Edition (New York: McGraw Hill, 2014), pp. 154–160.

7

THE CONFLUENCE OF BUSINESS INTERESTS, ECONOMIC THEORIES, GOVERNMENTS, AND EDUCATORS

Go to School to Learn Job Skills

Sparked by the fears of the Cold War and the destruction of World War II, world organizations were formed and economic theories developed that led to a world culture of education to serve the employment needs of global businesses. Born in the Chicago School of Economics, human capital and rational choice theory provided an argument that could be used to economize education and make its primary goal to be educating workers for a global economy. "Go to school to learn the skills that will get you a job" became the global clarion call of politicians, business, and educators.

There was no conspiracy that led to this result. It was a product of an entangled set of interests and ideas. The message given by some economists that education will cause economic growth and reduce income was quickly adopted by politicians and business interests. Faced with economic slowdowns or desiring to grow their economies, politicians could claim that investing in education would solve the problem without alienating the business community. Blaming education for economic problems is a safe path for politicians. Businesses endorsed human capital theory because it gave them an argument that schools should be teaching the hard and soft skills that they wanted. Since soft skills were high on their list of needs, human capital theory offered the opportunity for businesses to demand schools teach work habits and dutifulness wanted by global corporations.

Both politicians and businesses benefited from an economic theory that offered solutions to income inequality and failed or slow economic growth. Responding to complaints about growing income inequality, which might lead to progressive taxation for redistribution of wealth, it could be answered that providing a skill-based schooling would solve the problem. Politicians loved this solution because it didn't antagonize many citizens. More education sounds benevolent. Also, the argument that personal investment will lead to higher incomes became a justification in countries like the US to reduce government aid to higher education and rely on student loans to pick up the slack. This pleased bankers because student loans provided them with another source of income.

OECD became a major player in this tangled web of human capital ideas and global organizations. In its early form as OEEC and later as OECD, the organization focused on economic development and readily adopted human capital arguments. It pushed the human capital agenda by translating the call for schools to teach hard and soft skills into global tests. The launching of PISA in the 1990s and later PIAAC created a global academic Olympiad that pit nation against nation as to which education system was doing the best job in teaching work skills. In turn, the PISA's global Olympiad contributed to making human capital ideas sound like commonsense. The mantra became: invest in education and educate students in the right job skills and the economy will grow and income inequality will be reduced.

World Bank loans and policies created a confluence of corporate global interests, free market economic and rational choice theories, local education leaders, and local politics. Loans were to support education initiatives that would give local populations the knowledge needed to make choices in a free market, to become politically empowered, to stop the misuse of Bank loans, and to have the skills to join the world's workforce.

The World Bank joined the race to measure skills by collecting data beginning in 2012 for its Step Skills Measurement Program. Loaning money to developing countries, the Bank spread human capital education ideas which were sometimes in conflict with traditional schools created by European colonialists. It contributed to the mindset that education was primarily an economic tool. Thinking like bankers, World Bank officials originally focused on educating local populations to ensure proper use of its loans to build local infrastructures. The conceptualization of education as an economic tool was sustained when it adopted the goal of making a world free of poverty.

In addition, the Bank further extended the economic function of education by declaring it a necessity for individuals to operate in a free market and a tool to end government corruption that was hindering economic growth. In this manner, the Bank was able to entangle the neoclassical economics of the Chicago School with its education loans. Pushing its free market and rational choice agenda, the Bank argued that education was necessary for making rational choices in a competitive market. Bank leaders saw lifelong learning as compensating for job loss resulting from competition and technological developments. Worried about corruption and misuse of Bank loans, the World Bank gave an economic function to empowering the poor. Theoretically education was to result in citizens demanding an end to political corruption.

Bringing together business interests and research, the World Bank economized knowledge with the creation of the Knowledge Bank. Now economic growth was seen as a function of the production of knowledge. The value of knowledge was to be gauged in economic terms resulting in a greater emphasis on education that contributed to technological advances. In colleges, liberal arts declined as money and students poured into math, science, and engineering courses considered important for economic development. Students were to be taught the knowledge supposedly needed for economic growth, and ideas that might result in greater social and economic justice were not emphasized.

The confluence of economic interests and education policies was strengthened with the founding of the World Economic Forum to represent the world's leading corporations. Its strategy of multistakeholder partnerships guaranteed business domination of local school policies by linking business to educators and government. Making knowledge a function of business interests, particularly in the exploding technology sector, the organization promoted the use of ICT in global schools.

The World Economic Forum's multistakeholder partnerships helped reinforce the mantra that education can cause economic growth and reduce income inequalities. In particular, this was achieved by the organization's creation of a Human Capital Report and a Human Capital Index. The Human Capital Index joined with OECD's PISA to enhance the global Olympiad to determine which nation had the best workforce. This competition was to enrich global corporations by supplying them with workers with the "right" hard and soft skills. In addition, the World Economic Forum introduced the idea of entrepreneurship education as another source of economic growth and poverty reduction.

The confluence of business interests, politicians, government officials, and educators resulted in the attempt to control the social capital of families. Families, despite the wide variety of the world's family structures, were to be changed to meet economic needs. While some sociologists in the US context promoted stay-at-home moms as important for a family's social capital, most global organizations promoted female education to reduce family size and ensure the entrance of women into the workforce. The global ideal was small families whose social interaction supported success for the family's breadwinners and the teaching of soft skills to children for their success in school and work.

Global corporations might applaud the soft skills advocated by economists like James Heckman and taught in preschools. What boss wouldn't want workers who are conscientious, efficient, organized, ambitious, work hard, control their impulses, and have a good work ethic? But what is missing in these soft skills? As I've suggested throughout this book the missing soft skills that seem to find no room in corporate work or in the market are compassion, altruism, and empathy; all key ingredients to initiating struggles for social justice. Economists, like Gary Becker, consider the choice of soft skills dependent on their economic efficiency with selfishness making markets efficient and altruism making families efficient.

What happens if this confluence of business interests, economic theories, governments, global policy organizations results in the economization of schools, families, and childhood? Will it result in families and schools educating obedient workers who blindly accept their economic position in life and any economic misfortunes without striking back? Will this become a world of the rich and poor where compassion, altruism, and empathy are simply considered as tools for efficiency in families and not as energizers for campaigns for social and economic justice? Will governments simply follow the dictates of organizations like OECD, the World Bank, and the World Economic Forum?

If this confluence of interests succeeds this could become a world of human worker robots and economic masters who live on a slowly deteriorating planet where the economization of the environment or, as it is called, sustainable development, results in human inaction to protect the environment and other species. Maybe, humans will join the ranks of other declining species which the World Wildlife Federation estimated in 2014 to be declining at a rate of 50 percent over 40 years, involving: "10,000 representative populations of mammals, birds, reptiles and fish. Two human generations; half the animals gone."[1]

Note

1 Michelle Nijhuis, "The WWF's report on the shockingly rapid decline in wildlife should surely move us to action," *The Guardian/Observer* (October 4, 2014). Retrieved from http://www.theguardian.com/commentisfree/2014/oct/05/wwf-report-wildlife-decline-should-make-us-act on October 10, 2014.

INDEX